The Music Learning Profiles Project

The Music Learning Profiles Project: Let's Take This Outside uses ethnographic techniques and modified case studies to profile musicians active in a wide range of musical contexts not typically found in traditional music education settings. The book illuminates diverse music learning practices in order to impact music education in classrooms. It goes on to describe the Music Learning Profiles Project, a group of scholars dedicated to developing techniques to explore music learning, which they call "flash study analysis."

Twenty musicians were interviewed, invited to talk about what they do, how they learned to do it, and prompted to:

- Identify key learning experiences
- Discuss their involvement in formal learning environments
- Predict how they see musicking practices passing to a future generation

The Music Learning Profiles Project offers a nuanced understanding of the myriad approaches to music learning that have emerged in the early part of the twenty-first century.

Radio Cremata is Assistant Professor of Music Education at Ithaca College.

Joseph Michael Pignato is Professor in the Music Department at the State University of New York, Oneonta.

Bryan Powell is Director of Higher Education for Little Kids Rock and Interim Director for Amp Up NYC.

Gareth Dylan Smith is Manager of Program Effectiveness at Little Kids Rock, New Jersey and Visiting Research Professor at New York University.

Routledge New Directions in Music Education Series
Series Editor: Clint Randles

The **Routledge New Directions in Music Education Series** consists of concise monographs that attempt to bring more of the wide world of music, education, and society into the discourse in music education.

Eco-Literate Music Pedagogy
Daniel J. Shevock

The Music Learning Profiles Project
Let's Take This Outside
Radio Cremata, Joseph Michael Pignato, Bryan Powell, and Gareth Dylan Smith

The Music Learning Profiles Project

Let's Take This Outside

**Radio Cremata,
Joseph Michael Pignato,
Bryan Powell, and
Gareth Dylan Smith**

Routledge
Taylor & Francis Group

LONDON AND NEW YORK

First published 2018
by Routledge

2 Park Square, Milton Park, Abingdon, Oxfordshire OX14 4RN
52 Vanderbilt Avenue, New York, NY 10017

Routledge is an imprint of the Taylor & Francis Group, an informa business

First issued in paperback 2020

Library of Congress Cataloging-in-Publication Data
Names: Cremata, Radio. | Pignato, Joseph Michael. | Powell, Bryan. |
    Smith, Gareth Dylan.
Title: The music learning profiles project : let's take this outside / Radio
    Cremata, Joseph Michael Pignato, Bryan Powell, Gareth Dylan Smith.
Description: New York, NY : Routledge, 2018. | Series: Routledge
    new directions in music education | Includes bibliographical
    references and index.
Identifiers: LCCN 2017043237 (print) | LCCN 2017045978 (ebook) |
    ISBN 9781315206301 (ebook) | ISBN 9781138635951 (hardback)
Subjects: LCSH: Music—Instruction and study. | Alternative education.
Classification: LCC MT1 (ebook) | LCC MT1 .M98723 2018
    (print) | DDC 780.71—dc23
LC record available at https://lccn.loc.gov/2017043237

ISBN: 978-1-138-63595-1 (hbk)
ISBN: 978-0-367-60729-6 (pbk)

Typeset in Times New Roman
by Apex CoVantage, LLC

Contents

Series Foreword

The *Routledge New Directions in Music Education Series* consists of concise monographs that attempt to bring more of the wide world of music, education, and society—and all of the conceptualizations and pragmatic implications that come with that world—into the discourse of music education. It is about discovering and uncovering big ideas for the profession, criticizing our long-held assumptions, suggesting new courses of action, and putting ideas into motion for the prosperity of future generations of music makers, teachers of music, researchers, scholars, and society.

Clint Randles, Series Editor

Preface

With this book, the authors introduce the Music Learning Profiles Project (MLPP) and its methodological approach, one we call flash study analysis. Flash study analysis is a method that draws heavily on extant qualitative approaches to education research to develop broad understandings of music learning in diverse contexts. We view the MLPP as an international collaboration that is ongoing and will continually grow. The MLPP exists to collect and document large numbers of flash studies exploring music experience and music learning in various contexts that fall outside traditional school music education.

In Part I, we introduce and contextualize our work, provide rationales for the MLPP and for the flash study approach, and describe the methods employed in the project. In Part II, we present a collection of 20 flash study analyses. These preliminary profiles form the basis of the MLPP database, a repository of flash study profiles we intend to make available online following the publication of this book. In Part III, we consider the implications of the MLPP for music education research and practice, as well as for closely related areas of research and practice.

A key aim in presenting this work is to invite others to contribute to the repository of flash study profiles we have begun to amass. As noted, we intend to provide an online MLPP database, upon which colleagues in music education, ethnomusicology, and related sociocultural research disciplines can draw. Upon establishing the database, we will encourage other researchers to contribute flash study profiles based on the methods described in this text. By inviting such contributions, the MLPP hopes to democratize research to include more diverse experiences of music learning. Information regarding the MLPP and instructions for submitting flash study analyses for consideration and inclusion in the MLPP flash study repository can be found at mlppflashstudies.org.

Part I   Taking It Outside

Introducing the Music Learning Profiles Project

The Music Learning Profiles Project (MLPP) is an international collaboration to collect and curate a large number of studies exploring music making and music learning in a variety of contexts. The MLPP is concerned with "the continued importance of opening up what we conceive to be 'music education'" (Green, 2011, 19). Rather than using 'alternative' learning processes, that is to say rather than bringing (for instance) popular music learning models into school music programs, our interests encouraged us to look outside, beyond the schools, for more particular modes of music learning, knowing, and doing set apart from school learning. Consequently, most of the music learning described in this text occurs primarily outside of traditional school or music education contexts. Our hope in this project is to learn and to provide opportunities for others to discover and understand more about such learning phenomena and the particularized bodies of knowledge—musical and cultural—that they engender, with a view then to these understandings being woven into informed practice in music classrooms.

School and college music education around the world are dominated by the hegemony of Western art music, and, to a lesser extent, jazz (Bull, 2016; Powell, Smith, and D'Amore, 2017; Spruce, 1999; Wright, 2010). Performance and appreciation of these two traditions have developed discrete pedagogies, supported and maintained by a vast literature, including instructional traditions and 'methods' that Benedict (2010) and Green (2008a) critiqued for creating and perpetuating exclusive cultural contexts, 'authentic' only unto themselves. Randles (2013), Kratus (2007), Williams (2007), and Mantie (2014), among many others, have criticized this prevailing paradigm. Allsup (2010, 220) observed that, "considering the diverse array of music that is accessible in today's global world, it is surprisingly easy to figure out what counts as official knowledge among music educators." Allsup was addressing a largely North American audience; however, his observation could be made of many school music education traditions and contexts around the world. This book primarily addresses the myriad musics that exist *outside* of the official, institutionalized knowledge prevalent among many school music educators (Berger and Luckman, 1967; Hebert, Abramo, and Smith, 2017). It is with the practices and knowledges characterized by diverse experiences of musicking (Small, 1987) in ways intrinsic to those musics outside of normative school music education that we are concerned in the work of the MLPP.

Throughout the music education profession in the academy, 'other' musics and musicians do not have the educational capital or, thus, the cultural capital (Bourdieu, 2005) that they do outside of institutions, in non-school contexts. For example, Kallio (2015, 2017) notes that popular music education can sometimes be censored in ways that simultaneously legitimize certain musics through the reinforcement of moral boundaries, and delegitimize others, deeming them inappropriate. The authors believe that music learning in *all* contexts should be valued and included in discussions central to overlapping the disciplines of music education and ethnomusicology. In countries with long-established music teacher education (or training) systems, such as the US, Canada, and the UK, it is perhaps inevitable that highly evolved pedagogies in a couple of narrow traditions should have necessarily excluded others. Goble (2010) noted some US music educators presently appear to be in need of instruction on principles of democracy and the appropriate uses of music. However, as global populations diversify, as employment needs change, and as music education continues to struggle to maintain its place in schools in numerous territories, we propose the MLPP as a timely project to help bring to school and college music education broader and deeper understandings of the diversity of musicking and music learning practices in the world. We should emphasize here that we are not suggesting that current school music practices are inferior to largely 'outside' practices; rather, we aim to draw attention the breadth of musicking that is often excluded from school contexts. The principal aim of the MLPP, then, is to 'take this [music education] outside'—to appreciate and to help nurture genuine engagement with music learning in all of its marvelous and abundant manifestations.

A key impetus for the project derives from observations of the trend that participation in school music education in the US (where the four authors are based) is declining, and engagement with music after the high school years is at an historic low (Rabkin and Hedberg, 2011). Outside of school, however, creation, recording, and distribution of a wide range of musics proliferate in community centers, home studios, churches, and private teaching studios; at open mic sessions, jam sessions, peer listening sessions, and social exchanges about music; in recording or production studios, on bandstands in clubs and venues, and in DJ booths, in homes, basements, and garages (Waldron, 2013; Bennett, 2015; Pignato and Begany, 2015; IFPI, 2017; Pignato, 2017a, 2017b; Cremata and Powell, 2017). Increasingly, as Pignato (2017a) has noted, musicking and music learning occur in distributed, self-guided, asynchronous ways mitigated by social networks, streaming media, and other internet based platforms.

It can seem as though school music education exists in its own detached bubble, safe from the concerns of the real people whose lives and values it briefly engages or forever ignores in pursuit of its own propagation. While it is undeniable that positive music experiences are had by some (perhaps 'elite' or fortunate individuals) in schools, we are mostly interested in uncovering stories of music learning beyond the thin slice of school music education culture, with the purpose of including marginalized perspectives in the broader discussion.

Insofar as it looks beyond the profession's comfort zone, the MLPP is by no means a pioneering endeavor in music education. The project would have been unthinkable without the trailblazing contributions of, among others, Audubert et al. (2015), Azzara (2011), Barrett (2011), Burnard (2012), Campbell (2011), Green (2001, 2008a), Higgins (2012), Kaplan (1943, 1945, 1958), Mantie (2014, 2016), Partti (2012), Randles and Stringham (2013), and Söderman and Folkestad (2004). Particularly influential studies include Bennett's (1980) sociological analysis of becoming a rock musician and Campbell's (1995) ethnography of music learning in a teen garage band. Green (2001) profiled the ways in which groups of popular musicians learned, including through haphazard, exploratory learning, social exchange, and mixing and matching methods and private tuition lessons in highly personalized ways. Similarly, Pitts (2013) used ethnographic methods to analyze the formative experiences of music teachers. Waldron (2013) explored online communities of music learners that exist completely apart from traditional notions of school music education. Each of these precedent works underscored the significance and prevalence of music learning outside the contexts of school-based music education.

We are responding to a tangible and increasing yearning in the music education community for a reflexive refreshment and re-invigoration of the profession from scholars and practitioners, to bring meaningful music experiences to all young people through the powerful means of the education system—not 'just' so that people enjoy better *musical* lives, but so that, overall, people's lives, self-esteem, and happiness might improve (Wright, 2010). Consequently, we advocate that these examples of lived music and music learning experiences should not be ignored, and should be available for the benefit of scholars, practitioners, and students in music education.

A Democratizing Orientation

We view this project as part of a larger drive towards making music education more democratic, to expand the possibilities of what music education (and particularly school music education) means for individuals and groups (Horsley, 2015; Allsup, 2016; Moir, Powell, and Smith, in press). As Lingard observed, "it is through pedagogy that schooling gets done," and we are concerned about experiences in and outcomes of school music education, particularly the "reductive effects on pedagogy" wrought by the high stakes testing culture in the US (2010, 168–9) and elsewhere, and the pervasive music competition culture (Mantie, 2014). These wider issues are discussed at great length elsewhere in the literature (e.g., Allsup, 2010; Benedict, 2010; Reay, 2010; Vogan, 2010; Smith, 2011, 2013b; Stakelum and Baker, 2013). As Barrett (2011) advised, "the investigation of diverse music education practices provides opportunities for music educators to question some of the taken-for-granted assumptions that have shaped music education" (5). We aim to challenge colleagues, guiding them to question their assumptions, and—crucially—moving beyond such (wholly worthwhile) critical appraisal of their work, to find ways to change music education for the better, as befits particular local contexts.

Research Methods

The MLPP relies on classic ethnographic case study research techniques, primarily interviewing (Berger, 1999; Merriam, 1998; Seidman, 2006; Spradley, 1979) and informal and formal observations (Creswell, 2007; Lincoln and Guba, 1985; Stake, 1995; Yin, 2003). Such qualitative methods afforded us in-depth understanding of participants' music learning experiences, richer than might be garnered through other methods such as surveys or questionnaires. Interviews were semi-structured, with each member of the MLPP team using the same standard 13-item questionnaire developed by the authors (see Appendix A). Interviewees were asked to talk about what they do, describe how they learned (and learn) to do this, identify key learning experiences, talk about involvement in formal or school learning environments, and discuss how they see their particularized musicking practices passing to future generations.

To date we have worked with musicians active in domains external to mainstream school music education contexts; opportunities for data collection, potential participants, and insights therefore often arose spur of the moment, out of particularized cultural contexts, for example in clubs, in studios, or at social gatherings (Becker, 1973; Smith, 2013a). Consequently, we drew on a certain authenticity and on shared understandings as musicians

(Feleppa, 1986), conducting ethnographic study as participant observers, that required types of informal, dynamic, and conversational exchanges that often yielded valuable data, leads for additional participants, and deeper, more nuanced understandings of the varied contexts represented in this text. As musician-researchers, then, we shared with participants what Tiryakian (1973) called a "we-pole" (193), an assumptive frame of reference (199); the authors' collective backgrounds in the recording industry, music production, touring, performing, and promoting music afforded us a large network of contacts for generating leads. In addition, each of us teaches and actively researches popular, alternative, or informal modes of music making.

Stake's (1995) notion of collective case study, where researchers select several research sites, informed our approach. We selected initial participants known to us as peers through our own music-making networks, and through contacts in local, regional, national, and international music scenes. Potential participants were deemed eligible for inclusion if they were known to make music or musics not traditionally included in institutional settings. Using a kind of snowball sampling approach—whereby participants recommended further potential interviewees, and we looked to others in our own and one another's networks (Morgan, 2008)—led us to divergent characters, differing perspectives, idiosyncratic narratives, and music learning experiences often contrasting, contradictory, and highly particularized. We have extended the plurality proposed by Stake to a larger number than typical in traditional case study approaches. The MLPP brings together a multitude of flash study analyses, each a brief profile of an idiosyncratic musician and music learner who obtained substantial bits of musical knowledge at least partially outside formal institutions. Currently, the MLPP has compiled 30 flash studies (20 of which are analyzed in this book). We anticipate that this number will grow considerably as we continue with the project, invite more contributors, and tap into the networks of our participants, many of whom have provided leads and entrée into their communities. Given the established nature of their professional names, including a number of stage names, *noms de plume*, and preferred nicknames, the researchers sought permission during the institutional review process and from each of the participants to use their actual names. So, the names herein represent the names by which participants are widely known. Each of the participants is active in their geographic territory as well as online.

Flash Study Analysis

Music learning outside of traditional music education contexts represents a largely unexploited and seemingly endless font of potential data. The enormity of the potential cases necessitated succinct, rapid data collection and analysis that would allow us to amass a larger collection of profiles reflective of some of the diversity of that music learning. Merriam (1998) and Stake (1995) suggested using comparative case studies coupled with cross-case analysis as a means for developing profiles reflective of complex, ever changing social contexts. In order to ensure findings are "worth paying attention to," Lincoln and Guba (1985, 290) encouraged case study researchers to undertake "prolonged engagement" and "persistent observation" (307). Such recommendations hold true for in-depth, protracted case studies indicative of particularized contextual knowledge. We deliberately adopted a rather different approach.

We have adopted the term 'flash study analysis' to describe our approach. 'Flash' suggests a moment of illumination, akin to the flash of a camera or a streak of lightning across the evening sky. No single flash reveals much in and of itself. Collated, however, many flashes can illuminate much more, providing a richer portrait than any single photograph, or greater expanses of a landscape than a solitary flash of lightning. A flash study analysis is a short, written case study. Whereas case studies traditionally go into great depth (Robson, 2011), a flash study analysis is kept to a maximum of 2,000 words. Compiling many smaller profiles has generated a substantial pool of data from which we have begun to draw nuanced understandings of the myriad approaches to music learning extant in and emerging from the early part of the twenty-first century.

Each individual author/researcher decided what from the interviews and observations was important to include, in line with practices established in interpretive phenomenological analysis (Smith, Flowers, and Larkin, 2009). Coding was undertaken iteratively by each of the researchers, as we listened to recordings of interviews, transcribed the participants' words, and condensed the data into flash study analyses. Reviewing the analyses between us, we discussed intersections and commonalities, and collectively reduced an exhaustive list of over 40 codes into various themes presented later in this text. The collection and our understanding of the themes will likely expand and change over time. Further, we recognized "a third hermeneutic level [for] the imagined reader . . . trying to make sense of the researcher making sense of the participant making sense of X!" (Smith et al., 2009, 41). Since the researchers' biases and judgments become a research tool with which to analyze and interpret the data, Merriam (1998) suggested that researchers explore and explicitly provide a critical self-reflection regarding their assumptions, worldviews, biases, theoretical orientation, and relationship to the study that may affect the investigation. While, in the interests of concision, we have not provided accounts of such reflexivity in this text, it is precisely this activity that underpins and informs the interpretation and coding of data as described.

Before a flash study analysis is considered finished, it is shared with the participant for approval, as a requirement of the IRB-approved research ethics process. While there are obvious limitations to such an approach, there are also significant strengths, as we have indicated. The MLPP is interested primarily in extra-institutional musicking and music learning, two phenomena which, for the participants, are often not distinct. In the analyses, we thus tend to focus on data concerning these aspects of musicians' experiences to the exclusion of other elements. Individual flash profiles fall short of Lincoln and Guba's criteria for prolonged engagement with case study participants. We acknowledge this distinctive characteristic of our approach and assert its value as a key component of the MLPP. Collectively the 20 flash study analyses in this publication, along with hundreds or eventually thousands in the corresponding online repository, could illuminate a great deal. Also, as we discuss further below, this burgeoning collection of flash profiles should allow us and other researchers to piece together larger, macro understandings of music learning in and across immensely varied contexts: to take "the simple precaution of holding before [our minds] contrasting experiences" in music learning (Dewey, 1916). The flash study approach we are establishing here has possible potential to be utilized in other disciplines and fields as a new way of data gathering in qualitative research contexts. The emphasis on multiple flashes and plurality of perspectives, rather than deep case studies, might be useful in many domains of research, such as gaining insights into practices across the arts. One of the exciting features of the MLPP in its present and (we hope) future forms is that data can potentially be interpreted under many themes—according to readers' or researchers' disciplinary or cross-disciplinary orientation—thereby affording new insights with each interpretation.

Utility of the Music Learning Profiles Project

In collecting, analyzing, and presenting profiles in this text and in a forthcoming online repository, we hope to create a database for, and a community around, stimulating discussion primarily within the field of music education, regarding what might constitute valuable music learning experiences. We foresee collaborative discussions, ongoing and generative of new leads for potential participants, expanded awareness of myriad approaches to music learning practiced around the globe, and deeper understanding regarding commonalities, differences, trends, and anomalous individual possibilities that emerge from the flash study analyses. By hosting data primarily in an open-access online database, we aim to keep the data alive. Analyses should change, or be able to change, as more flash studies of cases are added. Hopefully then understandings, derived from analyses, could be incorporated into discussions affecting policy and curriculum decisions in music classrooms and in music teacher education contexts, democratizing music education access and practice.

In July of 2014, the authors presented the core elements of the MLPP during a workshop session at the 31st International Society for Music Education World Conference in Porto Alegre, Brazil. That session yielded valuable input from the scholarly community in music education and strongly suggested that colleagues would seek to contribute to the MLPP and to search the online repository. Prior to and since Porto Alegre, we have also presented the project at other conferences and symposia, continuing to gather feedback on and support for the MLPP. For the present, we invite other scholars, including graduate students, to contribute to the online database, which will be curated by the authors currently comprising the MLPP. We will provide a template for construction and submission of flash study analyses to ensure sufficient similarity for comparison. The MLPP database will have applications as a research tool and as a teaching and learning resource for master's and doctoral level music education scholars, for undergraduate pre-service music teachers, and for students in elementary and secondary school settings.

Scholars in music education, ethnomusicology, popular music studies, cultural studies, and related fields might use the database in much the same way as they engage with traditional collections of case study analyses—to gain particularized knowledge in regard to each of the participants. The breadth of cases in the MLPP also offers opportunities for a level of consideration that transcends the particularized contexts of individual profiles. Eventually, scholars will be able to cross reference the profiles in the MLPP database, in pursuit of macro level understandings of music learning as it occurs outside traditional music education contexts. Faculty teaching graduate seminars in music learning, informal learning, popular music, modern band, alternative music education, and qualitative research methods could incorporate the MLPP into their courses as a methodological model.

The database offers profiles of music learners and learning that are increasingly relevant to participants in contemporary music education. Many of the musicians profiled in the MLPP database resemble younger musicians likely to be encountered by—or even to be—graduate students, including those already working in the music education profession. We encourage submissions from students that profile discrete instances of music learning and that may thus provide emerging researchers with a path toward peer-reviewed publication. Finally, pre-service (trainee) teachers might learn from the MLPP about musics and musicking all too often overlooked in their studies. Like their graduate counterparts, pre-service music teachers will likely encounter or be musicians who share characteristics, traits, and similar experiences with musicians cited in this book and in the nascent database. It is our hope that pre-service teachers will use the MLPP database beyond their own courses of study, as they enter the profession and/or embark upon multi-faceted careers as musician–educators.

Part II   Music Learning on the Outside

A Collection of Flash Study Profiles

Participants

The following biographical sketches provide background on preliminary participants in the MLPP. Each of the participants is active in their geographic territory as well as online. Given the established nature of their professional names, including a number of stage names, *noms de plume*, and preferred nicknames, the primary investigators sought permission during the institutional review process and from each of the participants to use their actual names. So, the names herein represent the names by which participants are widely known.

Gavin Hammond is a musician based in London who takes pride in functioning outside of the mainstream music industry and is inspired by "punk, [which is] about DIY, is anti-professionalism and yet maximum content." Almost entirely self-taught, Gavin has worked creatively in music performance, photography, film, iPad app development, audio production, print editing, copy-writing, and songwriting.

Jacqueline Mannering is a 21-year-old musician from London, England. She has been a YouTube guitarist for six and a half years (as of September 2013), and has been labeled as a "heavy metal guitarist" who "just fell into that category" because "I like to play fast." Her learning experiences were hybridized (Smith, 2013a), incorporating formal and informal practices (Green, 2002).

Rod Melvin is a pianist and singer based in London, and has earned a living as a performer for 40 years. He plays piano every day, mostly in residencies in restaurants and private members' clubs, and often also sings. Rod took lessons in classical piano as a child and has since learned by ear and "on the job."

Anthony 'The Twilite Tone' Khan, a native of Chicago, has produced and written music under the names Ynot, 2 pc. DRK, Master Khan, and Great Weekend. The Twilite Tone explained his work: "I use the mechanism of music, whether it's production, or songwriting, or . . . being a conduit of the music . . . spinning or playing records and weaving them into a tapestry to tell a story."

Intikana Kekoiea, a Boriqua hip-hop artist, grew up in the south Bronx, one of New York City's five boroughs and the geographic location most frequently associated with the birth of hip-hop culture (Chang, 2005; Katz, 2012). Intikana best described himself: "I am a poet, an educator, a film-maker, a photographer . . . Everything I do . . . is through the lens of hip hop."

Amia 'Tiny' Jackson is "a recording artist, photographer, songwriter, radio show host, DJ, MC, and a student" at a small liberal arts college in upstate New York. Born and raised in Brooklyn, New York, Tiny Jackson presents as a natural entertainer. She hosts a hip-hop radio program that has generated a cadre of fans "in New York but all over too, like in other parts of the world."

Andy Krikun is a singer/songwriter, rocker, and educator whose musical experiences took him through the rock club scene in Los Angeles and New York, to graduate school, and later to teaching rock ensembles at a community college. Andy's focus now is on facilitating musical experiences for his students so that they might find their love of music.

DeVeor Rainey is a music educator, musician, and composer. Born in 1966 in the South Bronx neighborhood of New York City, DeVeor's musical learning journey has taken her from listening to the radio as a little girl, through the birth of hip-hop, to teaching music in an East Harlem public school.

Sean McPherson is a music educator and the co-founder and bassist of the Twin Cities hip-hop group Heiruspecs. While he values the informality of his hip-hop education, he believes he could have been better prepared for a career as a hip-hop artist if his formal education offered curriculum that considered the career demands of a professional outside of the academy.

Shana Falana is a singer, songwriter, and performer living in New York's Hudson Valley. She leads a band that bears her name, Shana Falana. Shana's music falls into "four distinct genres . . . silly pop," "dream pop," "ethereal . . . vocal driven, spiritual music," and "psychedelic, shoe gaze rock."

Neville Peter is a gospel musician dedicated to deep spiritual convictions. His music education has brought him from his first teacher, "the radio," to the small churches of his Caribbean island through university studies in jazz, to recording studios and live stage, and back to churches that resemble those he grew up in.

Raymond Wise is a fourth-generation church musician whose roots extend to his great-grandmother, who was a radio promoter of gospel music. He learned music in the context of family and home life. Currently he is a professional gospel musician, teaches gospel music at Indiana University, and through the Center for Gospel Arts teaches people the practice of gospel music.

Jean Baptiste Craipeau produces music in virtual ensembles. He regularly posts videos of himself singing multi-part a cappella arrangements of his favorite music. In addition, his work on YouTube, performing with a virtual a cappella group called Accent, has garnered a following. Jean Baptiste describes Accent as six men in five different countries.

Truth Universal, a native Trinidadian and resident of New Orleans, grew up in a rich and diverse musical milieu. A hip-hop artist, he most strongly identifies himself as a black American with African roots, and many of his rhymes today are postured around social justice themes from a marginalized Afrocentric perspective.

Jay 'J-Zone' Mumford does "a little bit of everything" out of necessity, curiosity, and quickly shifting focus. "In order to make a living, to survive, to get by," he's had to learn bits and pieces of engineering, producing, drumming, rapping, and negotiating the music business in pursuit of his career in hip-hop producing beats.

Jakub Smith has had a long and varied career as a bluegrass musician. Learning from growing up in a "bluegrass family," Jakub has expanded his musicianship by traveling the Appalachian folk music circuit "from North Carolina to Kentucky to West Virginia to Virginia, even up to Pennsylvania in Gettysburg, going to different bluegrass festivals and meeting people."

Robert Ray Boyette, known online as roboyette, started emulating drum rhythms using his mouth and voice "somewhere around six years old." What started as "original, unorthodox" vocalizing along with Robert's favorite music evolved into a highly idiosyncratic practice, "vocal percussion emulation of prog and metal drummers." Today, Robert enjoys an online reputation as a master beatboxer, known for his vocal interpretations of progressive rock classics to hundreds of thousands of fans of progressive rock, beatboxing, and drumming.

Mike Amari, also known as 'Lovesick', is a singer, songwriter, guitarist, drummer, music producer, and the primary talent buyer for

BSP Kingston, a small music venue in New York's Hudson Valley, some 90 miles north of New York City. Mike has toured the US and Europe as one half of the psychedelic dream pop duo Shana Falana.

Jacquelyn Hynes is a musician, actor, teacher, and activist, and primarily a flutist. A theatrical perspective helps her to see the flute as a character or protagonist when she is writing and performing with the instrument. She has learned in hybridized ways, including earning an MA in Irish Traditional Music, on which music was learned entirely by ear.

Riduan Zalani is a Singaporean Malay musician who has toured the world playing drums and percussion with artists in an eclectic range of styles. He leads two professional ensembles in Singapore that perform, champion, and promote music of the Malay cultural tradition, and aims to raise awareness of Malay culture in his native country and internationally.

Gavin Hammond

Gavin Hammond is a multi-faceted, independent musical artist from England, who hesitates to self-define as 'professional', despite broad, deep skill-sets, due to an uneasiness around his impression that professionalism too often implies 'corporate' or commodification. He takes pride in functioning outside of the mainstream music industry, saying that "I often deliberately do things with the minimum 'professionalism', but the maximum possible artistic output." He says that "what I'm looking for is sufficient imagination, and sufficient skills to be able to execute that imagination" as an independent artist making artistic and/or political statements that may or may not provide an income. Gavin works and has worked creatively in photography, film, iPad app development, audio production, print editing, copy-writing, and song-writing. Each of the skills that he has developed has been acquired in order to strengthen his ability to create and distribute the music that he makes.

Gavin started making music in 1976, in a climate inspired by "punk [which] is all about DIY—punk is anti-professionalism and yet maximum content." He expresses a deep sense of pride and empowerment at being an independently functioning musician, drawing heavily on the DIY punk ethos (Gordon, 2012), for instance stating that "I'm doing music out of pure malice, to fuck people up, to prove that a talentless person from a shit town can be called an artist." This aggressive attitude to his work is accompanied or underpinned by his aspirations to improve himself; he says, "I am absolutely passionate about learning; I think life is a golden opportunity to be a better person, and music is the best guide." Gavin's music, identity, learning, and politics are all intimately connected in a symbiosis lived out through his career.

Since adolescence, Gavin has found musical engagement to be a nurturing activity that provides a place for contemplation, warmth, and comfort that nothing else has. Writing and performing music have moved him throughout his life in ways that other artistic and technical pursuits have not. Throughout the interview Gavin expressed a childlike wonder and joy at the power of music to move people, as well as deference for others whom he considers to be superior to him as musicians. He emphasized that music is called "play—it's fun, it's not called work"—he also speaks of moments of "magic" that happen when musicking.

Gavin's Career

Gavin's career has, to a large extent, been guided by the repeated realization that in order to make his music he needed increasing autonomy. This, in turn, required the learning of new skills, some of which he acquired through taking day jobs to fund his music-making. Gavin is keen on the principle of 'art for art's sake', to separate his music from the need to make money to survive:

> The things I've done for money I've often felt a bit sullied by, and the things I've done for love . . . I've had a wonderful, amazing time, I've met some great people. There's something honest about having to work for your money and then doing art for art's sake . . . I can't make any money out of music, or I choose not to, depending on my mood.

Key to Gavin's musical journey is the punk-derived mantra of "the truth— three chords and the truth."

He "left school at 16 and played in a band, and I worked on a building site and I got a drug problem, and I got thrown out of my band and my house." He then moved from Cambridge to London and played in bands there, improved as a musician through relentless gigging, and "discovered practicing" (unaware of scales and arpeggios, he worked on riffs from songs). He moved to Australia, taught himself to play and use a synth, formed an electronic band, toured and made records with them. Feeling the need for greater creative and expressive autonomy, he took a handful of lessons in voice and finger-picking guitar technique, practiced obsessively, and then toured for six years "up and down Australia" as a solo folk artist playing three gigs a day. He wanted to make his own records, so lied his way into a job as the editor of a music magazine where he interviewed successful producers and engineers about making records. Based on their advice, he borrowed and saved up to buy equipment, experimented in his own studio, and "blagged a couple of audio courses through the magazine." He then began to produce his own records, and to help other musicians to "find themselves as an artist, and make that first artistic statement" in recorded form, something that he continues to do with musicians.

Learning

Asserting that "I am self-taught in every regard," the majority of Gavin's learning has been in the form of self-directed and informal learning, and reflecting upon and evaluating experiences. Gavin's ability as a journalist came to him easily because his father was a writer, and similarly with photography because his mother was a photographer—he had watched them both at work while growing up. He emphasizes the importance of "experience and practice" (in the sense of both doing, and repetition). He used to entertain himself as a child by making his own radio shows in his bedroom with two cassette decks and a turntable, making scripts and doing voiceovers. This approach of playfulness and experimentation with music is characteristic of Gavin's learning. The only two occasions on which he has taken formal lessons from teachers were when he took the series of guitar lessons "to learn the mechanics of finger-picking, from a left-wing union guy" and when he took a handful of vocal lessons to understand better the workings of his voice.

Gavin's career has been marked by several turning points at which he decided to learn new skills in order to achieve new goals. He has avoided studying at institutions of learning, and instead points to key moments of inspiration in everyday contexts. These include discovering his father's guitar, which "became my place of comfort," and through experimentation with which he began to write songs; the drummer in his band being "ruthless about time" led Gavin to the decision to spend a "year in my bedroom with a metronome," practicing playing his bass in time; hearing a one-eyed fisherman singing sublimely in a pub in rural Ireland led him to quit electronic music to pursue expression of purity and truth with his own voice as a folk singer; and wanting to "do something" for his long-time musical partner and backing vocalist culminated in writing and producing an album of songs as part of a multi-channel arts project embracing all of his skills and requiring him to develop more.

Gavin believes that 'knowledge is power', and that education should be about empowering people. He believes that "education is a wonderful opportunity in the hands of the good and the just," but that "education is an elite," closed sector of society. He feels that "academic institutions are about rinsing parents." He expresses reverence for education, but disdain for and distrust of the educational system in the UK, especially post-compulsory education, saying that "every experience I've ever had in an institution has been appalling . . . I am completely DIY, I don't believe in academic education—it's just a good way to make money for a lot of people." Recalling a Marxist perspective, Gavin feels that the societal system of which education is a part highlights the fact that "ordinary people have incredible strength that they don't have the time to tap in to." He points to the internet, particularly YouTube, as a source of immense potential for learning, despite the politics of education; he describes taking a job as a video editor despite having no skills in this area, and then learning on the job how to use industry standard video editing software from internet tutorials. For Gavin, who has always had the urge to learn, the key educational imperative is to "teach people to learn."

Skills and Attributes

Gavin maintains that "being fired is the best educational experience you'll get—every time I get fired from something, I need to get better at something else." Losing jobs has enabled Gavin to remain honest, focusing on what is important to him, rather than on what he can do to make money for 'the man'. He recalls how once "I ended up by accident working for Rupert Murdoch while playing folk music, and that's really confusing." Following this experience Gavin has tried to sell his skills only to charities and other organizations that appear to be working for the betterment of humanity. Thus, 'being fired' has been in several instances been key to Gavin identifying and focusing on the direction that he needs to take with his life.

Gavin sees the present era as one in which the boundaries between professional and amateur in terms of quality of practice and output are increasingly eroded, and as one that requires artists to engage with 'all channels'—an end towards which he has always strived. Now, using the internet and other contemporary technologies, Gavin writes and performs music, makes films, takes photographs, writes text, designs apps for tablet computers, and is able to market and distribute all of these outputs by himself. His current projects are deliberately 'all-channel'.

Passing It On

Young people today experience media convergence (Jenkins, 2006) as normal—they are used to music as video, interacting with touchscreens, viral marketing, and commenting via live RSS feeds. Thus, Gavin advises, "if you're young, don't do anything, just soak it all in, just be in your time. Try and live with kindness through your creative pursuits, try and do something for the benefit of others." In addition to this, he thinks it is essential to "be your own brand; don't copy everyone else—if someone comes to you, they know what they're going to get. Be authentic, and keep that voice going." Further, he counsels, "I've always punched above my weight—that's the best way to learn music, is to get in a band better than you . . . I like being not very good—it keeps me trying, it keeps me honest."

A blueprint for Gavin's career would require a person to "take drugs, hate the world, have no friends, and be stubborn at your own abilities or inabilities; then reform yourself from the drug addiction and get your shit together." Gavin is aware that he was raised in a society and amidst a zeitgeist that permitted his attitude and behaviors—he did not expect to find a job after leaving school, and was able to survive thanks to a generous welfare state. Gavin has "done a little bit of teaching, but generally [in these instances] I've been therapy or childcare for someone who doesn't really want to be a musician." He is, however, keen to help people, and to respond to anyone who asks questions or seeks guidance, leaving a legacy of enabling other artists. This is, he feels, essential in a world where "'productization'—commercialization of the universe—is all about separating people." Following a humanistic musical path offers a healthy alternative. Success for future musicians lies in being honest to oneself and in following pervasive spiritual teachings—"having a sense of a journey and a path . . . to ask the big questions, to feel the big love." Thus, for Gavin success is likely to lie in a combination of selfish artistic pursuit, and serving humanity with humility and kindness.

Jacqueline Mannering

Jacqueline Mannering is a 21-year-old musician from London, England. I initially met her four and a half years prior to conducting the interview for this study, when she was a student on the pre-college Diploma program on which I taught at the Institute of Contemporary Music Performance in London. We had been in touch once or twice since she earned her Diploma in summer 2009. I was keen to interview Mannering for this project as she seemed to be a rare case—a female electric guitarist making a name for herself. I was familiar with some of Mannering's YouTube videos, and was curious that a former shy, quiet, solitary student had crafted an online persona that appeared larger than life and almost cartoon-like, reminiscent of the manga cartoons of which I knew her to be a fan.

On her Facebook musician page Mannering describes herself as "Guitarist and Vocalist on YouTube." She has been a YouTube guitarist for six and half years (as of September 2013). She has been labeled as a "heavy metal guitarist" who "just fell into that category" because "I like to play fast." She has accrued over 45,000,000 views on YouTube, mostly of her playing guitar solos. She explains that "creativity on the guitar—soloing—is my main thing; there's something about it, it's just electricity sparking for me, when I'm playing a guitar solo". As well as playing guitar, Mannering is developing as a singer, using YouTube as the forum for gaining feedback to help with developing her voice (as she did with guitar). She also writes songs with a collaborative musical partner.

Mannering consciously plays a character in her online presence. She contrasts an overtly stereotypical femininity (pink, blonde or black hair, large, emphasized eyes, short skirts, tank tops) with stereotypically masculine musical performances (playing heavy metal guitar, soloing, playing fast and loud). Mannering's Twitter name captures the embodied contrast between the masculinity and femininity in her persona—she is @shred_kitten. As Mannering says, "I like to put out there the lead guitarist image and also frontwoman." She acknowledges that being a female in a traditionally male role as lead (and primarily heavy metal) guitarist "worked to my advantage—it was rarer at the time to see a girl guitarist" (in reference to when she began her YouTube career in 2006). However, for Mannering her image is situated within a popular music ethos of needing to be noticed, rather than being crafted in a deliberately gender-conscious manner. She explains:

> if I was a guy I'd probably think of something else to get views, rather than the image of a girl playing guitar, 'cause with music the image does draw you in . . . pop music is all about the image . . . people see what they want to see.

She perceives her character to be fluid and changeable with different videos, since "from moment to moment people are different, so it's hard to stick with one thing."

Although endless promotion of oneself as an international video music star could be construed as narcissistic, Mannering displays no such trait, revealing instead a generosity and desire to share: "I always try and put an emotion behind it; that's the important thing about music—it connects people emotionally and without that then it's just kind of dead." She "definitely want[s] to go to the top with [her] music," which would mean playing

> a massive show and giving all the money to charity and having all the people in the audience connected . . . playing a show does something special that's beyond our current understanding as human beings, something like another sense, almost.

Jacqueline's Career

After initially wanting to play drums and having this idea rejected by (musical and otherwise supportive) parents concerned with the noise, Mannering made a slow start at the age of 11 on acoustic guitar, which she "hated." When she heard Brian May playing, this ignited her desire to play solos on electric guitar. Mannering has now been playing guitar for ten years, and has been uploading videos of her playing for six. This began with posting videos for fun to her friends, one of whom told her that girls can't really play guitar and challenged her to play the internet classic "Cannon Rock" by Jerry C. She posted a video of herself playing the start of this, and, following her father's advice, posted it on Yahoo! This resulted in it being featured on Yahoo!'s homepage, and led to over 500,000 views in one night in 2006 (the total stood at over 670,000 on 9/11/13). Her development as a musician since then can be traced through her videos; she has "accidentally shown my progression as a musician throughout my YouTube videos." Mannering says that this shows "anybody can do it," and appears convinced that she is unexceptional, having merely tried hard and managed to catch people's attention.

Mannering does not earn a living from her YouTube career, but earns regularly from it through advertising and testing products; she has also secured endorsement deals where manufacturers of guitars and guitar pick-ups provide her with equipment free of charge in order to benefit from having their wares associated with her. At the time of the interview, Mannering had just begun to work with a producer in London on material for her solo project, using songs that she has written—an opportunity that she describes as "a dream come true." She is interested in teaching guitar and has considered doing this in the traditional manner of one-to-one lessons in face-to-face, real-time contexts, but said that she felt too disorganized to follow a particular method or plan. She has given voluntary guitar lessons at her old secondary school, where she "showed some of the students how to shred a bit," and has recorded video content and uploaded this to YouTube to be viewed as instructional material.

Learning

Mannering's learning experiences have been hybridized (Smith, 2013a), incorporating a mixture of formal and informal practices. She formed bands ('rock'-instrumentation ensembles) at school, but "had trouble finding people who had the same goals . . . the same desires musically as me." She has never had a regular guitar teacher, instead taking one-off or occasional lessons with local musicians and teachers, but has not done so for several years. When attending London's Institute of Contemporary Music Performance for one year after leaving secondary education, she learned from her teachers "their story . . . their experiences as a musician, rather than what was in the book." She also placed great value on the opportunities presented by the curriculum at the Institute to perform each week in bands a range of repertoire from the popular music cannon.

Music in compulsory education she found, by contrast, to be "boxing people in, rather than letting them free to be creative"; thus, she learned guitar largely by "watching guitar lesson videos on YouTube, jamming alone and messing around." Explaining the value of attending local gigs and watching YouTube videos, she says that "watching players I admire . . . eventually bits of that mix together and create whoever I became as a guitarist." She taught herself "what you see on YouTube," and has taken lessons in "music theory, scales, chords, all of that"; she is teaching herself to improve her sight-reading.

Skills and Attributes

Mannering believes the requisite skillset for working as a YouTube guitarist and front-woman to be more in the realm of 'life skills' than specifically musical-technical accomplishments. "To become who you want to be, it only takes the experience and knowledge and confidence to do it, and one day you'll reach a point where you can just do it," she says, adding that "playing in a band is a good experience, getting out there, gigging, just doing everything that you can." She states that one needs "to be able to work on your own and also as part of a team," and that to have "no expectations, and you can't lose." She emphasizes the need to have "no ego when you post something" and not to give in to perfectionism, to which there would be "no end—knowing where to draw the line is important" so that one acknowl-edges one's shortcomings. The most important factors in achieving success are "not letting the hate (worry over negative feedback via YouTube com-ments) get to you," because "anything that can be said, will be said," and "having the confidence to play—whatever builds up your confidence to be a player."

Passing It On

Mannering says that the path to becoming a YouTube guitar sensation is:

> YouTube . . . 'cause the internet has everything . . . the best thing to do if you want to learn to do something is to throw yourself into it. Post videos online and get feedback, take the constructive criticism . . . learn from what you do . . . for me anyway I'm constantly improving, there's never a point of stopping! Definitely, it will never end.

She states that the primary method for pursuing a profile as a YouTube gui-tarist and vocalist such as herself is to "start uploading videos"; this is not something that Mannering did *after* she had, in her view, become a mas-ter guitarist. Rather, her YouTube channel represents a way of being and becoming a guitarist, a mode of learning that she has undertaken 'on the job'. Her story embodies the reciprocal, symbiotic model of passive and active learning and identity realization described by Smith (2013a, 15–24). For Mannering, the future of electric guitar playing and soloing is in "creat-ing new sounds, taking what's been done and doing something interesting with it, moving forward, taking whatever technology we have and turning it into music."

Rod Melvin

> "My background is a love of playing the piano, love of songs, really, and to get paid to do that is ideal."
>
> (Rod Melvin, November 12, 2001[3])

Rod Melvin is a pianist and singer based in Walthamstow, northeast London. I met Rod through a mutual colleague in London's music scene. I have played drums on a handful of gigs with Rod in various ensembles over a ten-year period, at parties and concerts, and on recordings.

In order to have a license to sell alcohol after hours (UK standard alcohol licensing is until 11.00 PM), UK venues are required by law to offer live music, a requirement fulfilled in several London establishments by Rod Melvin. He has earned a living as a performer for 40 years. He plays piano every day, mostly in residencies in restaurants and private members' clubs in the capital, and often also sings. His solo performances are not concerts, but provide (often quite interactive) background music for socializing patrons, where the venues "make a feature" of the fact that there is live music on offer. Rod plays for parties and weddings; he writes and performs music for theatre shows at venues such as London's National Theatre, and fringe venues; he writes and performs music for film soundtracks, and has appeared as a pianist on film and on numerous music recordings. As the house pianist at London's Groucho Club, he meets, and performs for and with, celebrities and well-known people alongside other members of the public. He has performed and recorded with well-known 'alternative' mainstream popular artists such as Brian Eno, David Bowie, and Ian Dury (in Kilburn and the High Roads).

Rod's Career

Rod has been working in his current role since leaving the University of Reading as a Fine Art graduate in 1973. Rod's professional musical career began that summer with a stint at the Edinburgh Festival as part of a group from the university, playing music in a late-night drama production. The show was a critical success, leading to the group being booked for performances on London's fringe circuit and around Europe. Between tours with the drama group, Rod worked as the piano accompanist to a singer in a London club—a club attended by a young David Bowie who would "have sing-songs 'round the piano" with Rod.

Rod become a part of the alternative music and arts scene while a student at Reading, hosting and curating "fantastic parties" in a space in the art department at which bands including Roxy Music would perform.

Rod's band, Moody and the Menstruators (Rod was 'Moody'—the only male in the group), would perform as the support act, acting out popular songs with costumes and props according to the theme of a given party. Rod recalls that

> performance art was kicking off then, so we did all sorts of weird stuff— it was a very free and easy education; all your fees were paid . . . if you had an idea and wanted to do it, you just did it; there was very little formal structure, really.

He thus felt empowered and enabled to try out all manner of types of performance. This period of his life was instrumental in helping to establish the career that he has maintained.

Learning

Growing up in Cumbria, in England's northwest, Rod played piano from a young age. There was a piano in the family home, and his desire to play was inspired by his elder sisters; watching them play piano, he "naturally took to it,", believing "that's something I could do." He took piano lessons as a boy and learned to sight-read easily. Being "hungry for music," he learned a lot of old songs, "devouring songbooks, singing, and playing."

Rod had "very good piano teachers for the traditional classical music." Growing up, he had a great many opportunities to play music, and was encouraged to perform a wide variety of musics in public, including in local music festivals—experiences that helped prepare him for life as a professional musician. In addition to taking traditional, classical piano lessons, Rod has always been keen to learn songs of all sorts, including contemporary songs that were played "on the radio, and later, records." He has acquired a vast repertoire of popular songs spanning decades, through the classic "informal learning" (Green, 2002) practices of choosing songs to learn and learning these by ear.

Rod was given a funded place at a public (private) secondary school— Lancaster Royal Grammar School. The focus on music and the arts at the school enabled Rod to play piano every day for school assemblies—he would play duets with a music teacher, each of them seated at a grand piano. This provided Rod with valuable early experience of performing a wide range of repertoire to an audience on a daily basis. Having to time the music for the headmaster to arrive on stage, alongside singing and acting in theatre productions at the school, helped prepare Rod for a future working with multiple live performers. Rod recalls "good teachers" at the school, and that he was afforded "loads of opportunities to perform music" in public, such as at church services, for classical concerts, and in a popular music ensemble that he started with friends.

Skills and Attributes

Rod believes that there is no need for a person to earn a music degree in order to do what he does—he, after all, does not have one. He suggests that such a qualification would be no hindrance to working, though, since "there are people who have" music degrees that are working in a similar capacity to Rod. The ability to read music is necessary for "for different kind of jobs," while for Rod the essential skills for professional musicians like him are

> ear training . . . playing every day . . . it's good to have lessons to learn to read music and to get the basic technique . . . and then they can go and learn the kind of music they want to play.

Rod attributes his success in part also to "being curious about different popular songs—standards or classics, and keeping up with current music."

Rod emphasizes the need for sound pianistic technique, observing that often, where pianists have not acquired adequate technical ability through classical training, "people's technique is built around their limitations," resulting in a deficit in facility. He agrees with the maxim that playing the music of J. S. Bach on a daily basis can help performers at all levels to improve and maintain their skills. "The ability to play by ear" is an indispensable skill as well, as is a good memory for songs learned; Rod does not take sheet music or other notation to work with him, but instead has his repertoire memorized.

Since he works mostly as a solo pianist, Rod is responsible for providing rhythm, chords, and melody. Rod feels that his classical training helped him to gain this ability to play fluently with two hands, in a way and to a degree that pianists with different training may lack. Rod emphasizes the on-the-job nature of learning his craft, saying that "the good thing about what I do is that I do get to play every day . . . just from doing that, you get better, and you can try all sorts of different things out." The sense of an exploratory competence—wherein his ability permits experimentation—appears important in Rod's work. Rod feels that his success in his work comes from the fact that "what I really love is accompanying, 'cause I've always accompanied myself, from back when I was a kid."

Rod emphasizes a set of extra-technical and extra-musical skills that are central to his work. In his role he must have "an enthusiasm for music";

be able to "play by ear"; "be familiar with popular songs" for when people ask for requests; have "a willingness to play while people are not listen-ing—while they're eating, talking, whatever"; and "you have to read the room," i.e. respond through performance to the volume, energy, mood, etc., of an audience not engaged in active listening. Rod finds that "an interest in people is really necessary—more so than if you're just doing concerts, I think." Connected to this is the need to fit in with the 'feel' and the culture of the venue in which he performs. Clubs expect him to greet and welcome people, and "regulars get to know you, and like to chat . . . you have to be patient and tolerant [with drunk people]" owing to the late-night nature of Rod's work at the clubs (he usually finishes working at a club venue at 2.00 AM).

Passing It On

Observing that "there is definitely a demand for teachers," Rod is keen to engage with educating musicians. He has worked only a little as a teacher, and does not advertise or think of himself as a teacher. He has mentored people on short-term bases, such as the member of a popular boy band who wanted to be able to accompany himself singing songs in a bar. Rod

> worked out this diagrammatic way of showing him where to put his fingers (you know, like you have the guitar diagrams), and I got him an old piano to use for his flat [apartment], and then he got into it so much so that he used it to write songs with, so my job was done then . . . 'cause I got him the piano, that was the key thing, and having it there he began to use it.

Apparently, this boy-band musician had (abortively) taken lessons with sev-eral advertised piano teachers, and Rod was the first who had asked him what he wanted to achieve; other people had told this student that he would have to learn to read music, despite this being unnecessary for his goals. Rod likes the idea of working with adults, rather than working in a school, "tailor[ing] the programme towards what they need":

> I get asked an awful lot if I give lessons . . . you always have to nail down, well what is that the person wanted to do; like this person in the boy band didn't want to learn to read music, so that's a whole lot of time, you know, out of the way. I would like to do more teaching, but I haven't worked out for myself how I would best do it. I think I need a separate space, really.

In Rod's case it seems that the freedom from knowledge of a pianistic peda-gogy may be enabling his engagement with students in an intuitive and non-formulaic way. Rod also used to run a choir, "from my enjoyment of songs, really, and singing. I like encouraging people to sing."

Anthony 'The Twilite Tone' Khan

> My purpose is to communicate, inspire, and possibly give freedom via music, art, so called fashion, and multimedia . . . I use the mechanism of music, whether it's production, or songwriting, or . . . being a conduit of the music . . . spinning or playing records and weaving them into a tapestry to tell a story.

About The Twilite Tone

Anthony 'The Twilite Tone' Khan, born in Chicago in 1971, has produced music under the names Ynot, 2 pc. DRK, Master Khan, and Great Weekend. The Twilite Tone, often referred to as simply Tone, produces music in a variety of modalities, genres, and contexts. He writes songs, produces recordings, spins records as a DJ, and curates music for other performers and for cultural events.

Khan is recognized as a major figure in the history of Chicago's rich dance music culture, having cultivated his craft in that city's clubs throughout the 1990s. Tone's influence expands beyond the Chicago clubs. He has multiple Grammy® nominations, is a BMI Award–winning songwriter, and served as Music Director and DJ to Common. Additionally, Tone has written music with and produced albums for leading figures in contemporary music, including Kanye West, John Legend, Pusha T, and Big Sean, among many others.

Data Collection and the Developing DJ

Anthony Khan grew up primarily in Chicago and in Southeast Louisiana, locations that afforded him formative musical, cultural, and intellectual experiences. As early as 3 years old, Khan exhibited a penchant for following the records of the day:

> As a young child, I was so into it that my mother would gather people around to ask me about the top 10 or the top 20 on the radio. I think I was like three or four, or something like that, and I could tell them.

Tone's recall of the top radio records of the day reflected a kind of "research . . . collecting data" resulting in a carefully cultivated and idiosyncratic base of music knowledge that would inform his work for years to come. Tone explained:

> I started off with research, as a child, knowing top 10 records. It didn't stop when I was three. I constantly submerged myself . . . collecting

data and proof of what I thought was of value or great, [researching] and learning the music.

With each successive discovery, Tone's knowledge blossomed. The vinyl LP, the prevailing medium of Tone's formative years, the 1970s and 1980s, and the preferred medium of DJs the world over, facilitated the process:

> What's so beautiful about vinyl is the credits and the artwork. It's like you get inspired by the art. You have these colors with the art but also you learn who is the faculty of this record and then you see these names and when you go out to buy more music, you notice that the people that the faculty members who created the album that you love actually have albums themselves, which have additional faculty members who actually have albums themselves, you know? And it doesn't stop.

Where poring over album liners provided Tone with a who's who of recorded music, listening to albums provided a storehouse of knowledge about genres, production techniques, and an ever-expanding cache of sounds, samples, and inspirations:

> So you collect data . . . I'm able to grab a sample or a sound bite. I'll grab a record, I'll see an artist and I'll see where he wants to go and I'll grab a bunch of records that I feel are cousins to what they want to do as an example of where you can go. So it helps me in a lot of ways. So it helps me as far as actual material to create with, knowing records, and having data.

Chicago, Friends, Family, Influences

Tone's childhood and early stage career reflect the musical diversity and heritage of his native city, Chicago. He peppers his narrative with references to the influences of family, friends, and teachers, some of whom shine among the bright points of the constellation that comprise that city's musical heritage. When Tone was asked about influences, mentors, or teachers, he responded, often with deeply personal recollections:

> The first is my mom and just what she exposed me to, whether it was music or whether it was just media, period. I mean my mother exposed me to lifestyle and music and, like, I knew about people like Second City TV, and SNL, and Cheech and Chong, and Richard Pryor because of my mom, but I also knew about Earth, Wind and Fire, and Joan

Armatrading, and jazz, and dance, and just renaissance people; Gordon Parks, learning, just different things, you know; Elton John, just different things because of my mom and my family.

Others in Tone's family played important roles as well, and at least two ranked among Chicago's most-lauded musicians. Tone spoke about the influence of his cousin, Richard Davis, a storied jazz bass player, a noted pedagogue in classical and jazz bass, and a significant contributor to two of rock music's most influential recordings, Van Morrison's "Astral Weeks" and Bruce Springsteen's "Born to Run." In addition, Tone's uncle Hassan Khan, another bass player, provided encouragement, tutelage, and even tools of the trade:

> My uncle Hassan Khan, who's a great bassist and a visionary, he gave me equipment and he talked to me and I was able to look at him and be inspired by the things that he did and um, then, also his impact on, obviously, the legendary Chaka Khan, his sweetheart, whom he named Chaka, and them getting married.

Beyond his family, Tone drew influences from and sought out mentors among Chicago's dance music culture. He had been dancing from an early age and, in some ways, through dance, he found his way toward one of the genres in which he would eventually excel.

Dancing in Chicago, like other major US cities of the 70s and 80s, happened in clubs but also on the street as young dancers joined crews and danced in competitive battles. Tone explained the importance of 'battling' as a platform for performative expression but also as a kind of workshop for learning through competition, social exchange, and peer influence:

> So throughout my life, I've been dancing, whether it's dancing itself or dancing in a competitive sort of way, and I mean not necessarily formal dancing . . . like street dancing, or whatever, or, you know, dancing in the neighborhood, you know, people would what you call battle or be in competition with one another, who had the better moves, or whatever, and this helped to influence and to inspire the kind of music I make.

Tone's immersion in street battling corresponded with the development of Chicago's burgeoning House music scene. Chicago House developed in the mid-1980s and proved to be of greater influence than anyone at the time could have imagined (Church, 2010). For Tone, many of the early Chicago DJs provided role models, mentors, or willing collaborators:

> There were DJs coming out, and that really blew me away. I just saw myself being that guy behind that box, you know, pressing those buttons or turning those knobs. I literally had visions of that.

Much of Tone's knowledge derived from hearing what friends or respected associates, a few years older, maybe a bit further into the cultural mix of the period, recommended. Some were mentors, "big brothers," functioning like masters to Tone's apprentice:

> I had big brothers along the way that said, "Hey man, do you know about this? Do you know about that?" DJs like Steve Maxwell . . . being this sort of sensei type of person. This gentleman Frank Washington, these are older gentlemen in Chicago, who in Chicago have a lot of respect as far as like DJing. Steve 'Silk' Hurley . . . just different people that I've been exposed to, DJ Spinner, Rich Medina; great inspirations to me that I didn't talk to directly but I was in close proximity to like Ron Hardy, Lil Louis, I did talk to, he inspired me, Frankie Knuckles, Gene Hunt . . . so many, so many.

In addition to those big brothers, Tone drew on contemporaries. He came up with a cadre of peers—DJs, producers, and cultural provocateurs—each of whom, like Tone, developed an idiosyncratic style. Tone explained, "My friends helped me out, a lot. From my friend ReggieKnow or ReggieKnow Jolley, No I.D. (Dion Wilson), who's a great producer, to Common." Tone drew on younger artists as well, "even people that came after me inspired and motivated me and came up to me and acknowledged me and, you know, people like Kanye West, to even like his DJ Million Dollar Mano."

School Education as Point of Departure

For Tone, school music programs, particularly music classes at Chicago's Kenwood Academy and marching band programs and the marching band culture prevalent in Southeast Louisiana, also provided necessary training, a complementary skill set, performance experiences, and a framework for thinking about creativity, aesthetics, and style. Although most of Tone's narrative focused on learning outside of school music, he referred back to specific or important school music teachers: "Mrs. McGlynn . . . a vocal coach at Kenwood Academy . . . Mr. Watkins, that was junior high school, Davis High School." Tone explained some of the roles institutional music education played in his development:

> My education in the marching band situation was vast, man, because not only was I learning music, how to play an instrument, but I was learning how to have workability, in motion . . . it's like we're moving and we're creating dance and sequences and having to keep count. It's a certain amount of discipline, but it's a certain amount of freedom that you have to have within that.

School education played another, more profound, role in Tone's development. The rigidity of marching band, of traditional school music aesthetics, and of the emphasis on canonical repertoire formed a kind of framework for creative departure. Tone explained:

> You know, I wanted to be the drum major of the Southern Jaguar Marching Band. I wanted to be one of those guys, but that was one of my goals from the past. By the time I got there, I wanted to create music. I didn't want to be in the marching band anymore. It actually inspired me to want to rebel against convention and structure. Think outside of the lines or to color outside of the lines. But I also value that, I value that pressure for those lines being drawn, because out of that, I was able to come to a world of creation.

And yet those experiences remain important to Tone's sense of creative identity, a revelation of 'maturity' that prompted him to reevaluate the roles played by the rigidity of his formal education:

> So as a kid, as I rebelled against it, we circle back, don't we? We circle back to those things we rebelled against and look at them in a different context . . . Now I see it with great value. I'm glad. I'm glad that I had that as an institution to rebel against. I'm glad I rebelled and I'm appreciative that I can see that right now.

Great Weekend, a Purposeful Vision

Tone brings each of the seemingly divergent strands of his narrative together under the canopy of Great Weekend. Great Weekend serves alternately as a production alias, as the name given to club parties cultivated in Chicago, Los Angeles, New York, and other cities, and as a catch-all concept reflective of Tone's intentionality, of the purposeful vision of creative liberation hinted at in the epigraph to this profile. Tone explained:

> Great Weekend means freedom, or every day is Saturday. You achieve every day is Saturday is by knowing your purpose, doing your purpose, moment by moment. Once you're doing that, you have every day is Saturday. Time doesn't matter. There is no struggle. There is no grind. Even if you're working from sun up to sun up, you're doing *your* purpose; that is the thing that you would do every day for free, that you want to provide.

Intikana Kekoiea

> I am a hip hop artist from the south Bronx. I am a poet, an educator, a film-maker, a photographer . . . Everything I do . . . is through the lens of hip hop . . . I am a Boriqua, Taino hip hop artist, so my culture means a lot to me.

About Intikana

As one might gather from that introduction, themes peppered throughout Intikana's narratives reflected notions of place, of locus. His narratives illuminated a complex of spaces, locations, and particularized geographies from which Intikana derived poignant, albeit situational identities in the worlds of hip-hop, the Bronx, Boriqua culture, but also in his personal life, as schoolboy, son, college student, and community activist.

The Bronx

Intikana, born Anthony Martinez, grew up in the Bronx, one of New York City's five boroughs and the geographic location most frequently associated with the birth of hip-hop culture (Chang, 2005; Katz, 2012). Although estranged from his father, Intikana grew up very close to his mother, to her extended family, and to his largely Puerto Rican community. Intikana's childhood, including the story of his parents, a rekindled relationship with his father, and his earliest life experiences, has been thoroughly documented in the form of an autobiographical theatrical production titled *Penumbra*. Consequently, this flash profile focuses on Intikana's narrative as it relates to self-identify, music learning, and cultural knowledge.

From an early age, Intikana viewed himself as an artist, as a performer, as one for whom words, music, art, and movement would provide therapeutic comfort. The Bronx, New York City, and Boriqua culture informed Intikana's earliest identity development. Intikana explained:

> My first theatre performance, from what I can remember, I was seven years old; I did a theatre performance at a nursing home. It was a play and I played a character and it was like in the *Daily News* and there was like a little picture of me as a kid, and it was cool and that was like my first performance.

In addition to performing publicly in school and community productions, Intikana began writing at an early age, at first simply to write down or record thoughts, later to keep journals, and eventually to experiment with words, to express with words, and to make sense of himself, of the life and world surrounding him, and as a means of coping.

> You know, I would do journal writing here and there but it wasn't until I was about twelve years old which was when my grandfather passed, when he left, and considering how that transition was a little hard for me at that time, it became an opportunity for me to, I guess vent and kind of work my own self-therapy through writing so I started writing poems and from middle school into high school, I started writing raps.

Writing for "self-therapy" led Intikana to rapping. Rapping in social circles with friends, but perhaps more significantly, with adversaries, led Intikana to hip-hop.

Battling

Intikana began formulating much of his performance persona, often difficult to distinguish from his actual persona, in hip-hop battles, a long standing competitive exchange with roots in gang battling, later b-boy battling, and eventually battling between DJs and MCs (Chang, 2005). Intikana explained the importance of battling in the development of his craft, but also in the development of a "warrior spirit":

> Initially, [my rhymes] were just for me, maybe for my very close group of friends until, eventually, I got heavily into battling. Battling that's when in school, especially in high school, it was very prevalent, if anyone heard you rap it wasn't like you could just rap and make a song, it was like people were knocking on your door, while you were in class, waiting for you to come out so they could battle you. So, it was a very competitive atmosphere but it was also a chance to always be on your toes. It was . . . it was in many ways, exciting, like a warrior spirit. I learned a lot from those experiences and then eventually I had the opportunity to go to college, which I was very hesitant to initially, I didn't want to.

Feeling Apart

On more than one occasion, Intikana expressed feeling apart from, or othered by, institutional learning. He lamented a number of critical omissions in his elementary, secondary, and later collegiate education programs:

> I liked learning. It's just that a lot of what I was learning had not much to do with me. It had not much to do with my family, my surroundings,

my ancestry, nothing really. All from kindergarten to high school, I can't remember one class not even a course but like one single class. I can't remember one class that focused on Boriqua, Puerto Rican, quote unquote, studies. I don't remember one class on that.

Intikana often spoke of social inequity in education, and in regard to the social, political, economic, and cultural disenfranchisement of minority communities, particular of hip-hop culture. He explained:

It's really a cultural thing, power, money, resources. I mean, I've heard people criticize hip hop because [in mock voice] "you don't have enough musical accompaniment. You don't have no musicians. There's no real drums. You just samplin'." But, a lot of us don't have the money to get a big band the way we want to. I'm sure if we had the funds, the resources, we'd come up with crazy hip hop orchestras! But it's so hard to be able to get those funding sources, and especially when you use words like hip hop, people hear those words very differently and they're not informed on what they really mean, especially in a commercial world where governments, specifically, really focus on portraying this image that's not accurate, and not only is it not accurate but it's self-destructive to our youth, to our generation and so on and so forth that it becomes hard on the artists who do keep it true to the culture and keep it real to its roots.

Not surprisingly, Intikana increasingly works as a community activist, organizing educational programs regarding Boriqua culture, Bronx cultural history, social justice, and urban life. For Intikana, musical identity, and the skills, knowledge, and experiences that engender musical expression, at once reflected and subverted his status as other in the worlds of institutional learning.

Quest for Knowledge

Despite his status as other, Intikana continued to pursue education, in some cases, using the very institution from which he felt excluded in subversive ways and in pursuit of his own interests. Intikana described his days working as a work-study student employee in the college library:

In college, I remember, I used to also work at the library so I used to [chuckling], I was supposed to, you know, order, put the books in order and on all the different shelves or whatever, but a lot of times [chuckling], I would just get lost in the library like I was supposed to be doing these orders but I would start reading, I would pull random books from the shelves, whatever titles appealed to me, and I would read a chapter and then I'd put it back and I'd go to the next, you know, aisle and order more, you know put more books and then I'd find another title that called to me and then I'd pull it out and I read a chapter. A lot of them were, you know, I was just reading all these books. I just got . . . I would dip my feet in so many different spaces and areas of knowledge that it became exciting.

Going Outside

For Intikana, going outside proved a viable path toward finding a sense of musical self, and in the pursuit, to answer fundamental philosophical questions:

One day, when I was in the music library I was like, "wow, I wonder what they have on Puerto Rico, here." This is at the [college] library, and it was somewhat of a big sized library, and I went all over even to other areas beside music. I couldn't find nothing on Taino. I couldn't find nothing on my ancestors. It tripped me out because it made me think that we didn't have a history, no culture, no music. Here I was at college and, like, I didn't have a history.

So, when I'm looking to find myself in college, university, institutional settings, as a "young brown male," whatever that means, for me not to find myself in a library, which is supposed to be a resource of knowledge became this really weird [pauses], problem for me. It made me want to look elsewhere to find something about myself. I started looking on line, looking for books, and it made me think, like, you know the question that we all have to answer at some point no matter what artist you are, no matter who you are trying to reach musically, the one question we're all trying to answer is "Who am I?" "Who am *I*?" "Why am I?" Why am I who I am?" "Do I matter?" "Who have I been?" "Where do I come from?"

For those questions, Intikana, with a clear, purposeful intentionality, went outside, outside the corridors of the Bronx middle school where he first began battling other rappers, beyond the confines of his high school when he thought collegiate music studies would help him further his hip-hop aspirations, and, after being othered by omission once again, outside collegiate music studies in search of "poietic" spaces (Nattiez, 1990), where he might produce hip-hop recordings, sure, but much more, hip-hop expressions of Intikana Kekoiea, of his notions of Boriqua culture, of Bronx life, of his place in those worlds, in the world at large, of his humanity.

Amia 'Tiny' Jackson

> Honestly, what I would do . . . I wouldn't send them to a school, hell no!
> Y'all ain't gonna learn how to do hip hop in a school. I would send them
> to a . . . I'm looking for the proper word. I would send them to a damaged
> neighborhood and tell them write about what they see. I think that's the first
> step to hip hop.

About Tiny

Amia 'Tiny' Jackson is "a recording artist, photographer, songwriter, radio
show host, DJ, MC, and a student" at a small liberal arts college in upstate
New York. Born and raised in Brooklyn, New York, Tiny Jackson presents
as a natural entertainer, a personality to which many on her small upstate
New York campus gravitate. She hosts a hip-hop radio show, popular on
campus but also online via web streaming. Tiny's radio program has generated a cadre of fans "in New York but all over too, like in other parts of the
world." In addition, Tiny produces, promotes, and MCs hip-hop showcases
in New York City and in Central New York.

   Like many musicians active in this second decade of the twenty-first century, Tiny exhibits an entrepreneurial directedness, a clear sense of agency,
intentionality, and purpose. Her narrative links seemingly divergent endeavors into a comprehensive whole, reflective of her aspirations.

Learning to Rap

Tiny began writing rhymes and keeping a notebook of rap lyrics in her
Brooklyn, New York apartment. Her mother and her mother's friends would
talk, often about complicated, adult-centric problems like domestic violence, infidelity, substance abuse, or the challenges of raising children without adequate resources. The women tried to 'shield' Tiny and her siblings
with whispers, private code words, or by speaking in euphemisms. Tiny
listened intently, intuiting the gravity of the discussions; tuned in to the elder
women's consultations, she began writing rhymes. Tiny rhymed to process
the knowledge to which she had become privy, but also to declare, albeit
indirectly, "hey, I know what y'all been talking about." Tiny explained:

> That's basically how I started rapping; just from seeing things and hav-
> ing nothing else to do but write. You know, I didn't really have any
> other outlets to express what I was feeling, so I did it by writing raps.
> That's how I started. I wanted to rap about their problems to let them
> know, "I understand what y'all talking about." They used to come and
> just gossip, like, from watching people be abused, they come in talking

about being cheated on. That's what I rapped about for a lot of my life. It's about what I seen and how the other females were being treated.

Those early efforts astounded her mother and her mother's friends, a number of whom rhymed, wrote poetry, and privately rapped, an activity largely off limits to women in the 1990s. After reviewing Tiny's notebooks and overhearing her rapping, the elder women responded, providing a kind of public affirmation that at once startled and sparked Tiny's desire to become an MC:

> So I sat down, my mother, her friends, they were looking at me like, "What the hell you talking about?" I had just been writing about everything I heard from them. Like, yeah, "you, this is your problem right here. This is exactly your problem," and they was like, "Oh my god, you could really rap because this *is* my story." You know, I was able to share somebody else's story without them actually sharing it. It made them feel like, "That's exactly what I went through." So basically like telling them their story through different kinds of rap; and they were so amazed, and that's when I took it kind of serious.

One of the women, Tiny's aunt, only two years older, provided a formidable role model. Tiny explained the relationship: "I somewhat followed my aunt, she rapped too and is really good; very lyrical, nasty. Like, I'm good but she's, I'll say she's great; yeah, she's awesome."

In an effort to learn more, Tiny also consulted with her mother's boyfriend, the father of her brother and sister. The gentleman, a rapper himself, kept copious notebooks of rhymes, a practice which Tiny began to emulate as a way to save, edit, and refine her work:

> I used to like to read his books, you know? I never understood that it was a formula. I didn't understand like chorus, verse, verse, chorus, but I would listen to music, you know, and I would like study somebody else and I just picked up on it.

Most of her early learning stemmed from listening to her mother and friends confide in one another, hearing their words, reading their rhymes, studying their various modes of expression, reviewing her mother's boyfriend's notebooks, and listening to popular rap artists. Tiny described the process:

> It's not like . . . I mean, I never really had somebody sit down and teach me like a scale, like this is how you write a song. I never had that. You know, I didn't know you could like switch things around and do this

and that. I would just do things because I felt like I wanted to do it but I never really had somebody teach me skills, how to do things. It was just something . . . before school, I just taught myself. I never really sat down with somebody, like 'your gonna do this, this, this, and that.' It was more of a . . . I did it myself, I wrote raps.

Battling also played an important role. Tiny engaged in rap battles at school, at a local church, and, reflective of her indefatigable entrepreneurialism, organized rap battles on social media networks. She took every opportunity she could to learn from others and, where she thought she could "lend a bit of something," help aspiring MCs, particularly "females who don't get a lot of support." Occasionally, Tiny rapped at her high school. Public affirmation at school prodded Tiny to view rapping as a 'lifestyle', increasingly desirable as she became intoxicated by growing accolades and by the potential to affect change in others, to inspire, either through spiritual messages or through diversionary rhymes, or "turnt up, party music."

In Schools

After years of limiting her rhymes to close family and friends, Tiny rapped for a group of younger students at her high school. The students, Tiny's classmates, and her teachers encouraged further pursuit:

> Performing at my high school. I used to rap about god a lot. A lot of my raps is about god. I'll never forget this show I did where I was rapping about god and people was like, they had this school visit us, and people was like asking for my autograph, it was so weird. I was like "What the hell? You want my autograph?" I think that's when it struck; like, "Oh, I like this lifestyle." Like people really looking at me like, you know, "That was really good," and my teachers saying, "That song was very inspiring, was very moving." You know, seeing the reaction of my friends and the other kids. Maybe I could change them, or help them have fun despite their problems.

Tiny graduated high school and enrolled at an upstate New York technical school, where she played basketball on scholarship. On a lark, she joined some friends for a weekend visit to a nearby four-year liberal arts college. There, Tiny enjoyed the typical college weekend fun, but learned about something altogether new, studying music:

> I visited and then learned a little about the college, and was like "Oh, they got a music industry program? What? Music industry? You could

go to school for music?" Like, I never heard of that before. Like, "How can you go to school for music? Is that even such a thing?" You know? So I looked into it and applied. I'll never forget when I got accepted I snapshotted it, put it on Facebook, and emailed it to my mom.

Opportunities and Barriers at School

At school, Tiny found courses and opportunities for developing her MC skills. Of particular influence was a study abroad session in Ghana. While there, Tiny discovered soca music, the music of Bob Marley, and the diversity of African and African diaspora musical traditions. At the same time, feelings of alienation, frustration with the institution's general education requirements and prerequisites, and a paucity of hip-hop offerings irked Tiny.

Initially, Tiny pursued basketball, her theretofore priority. She encountered what she perceived to be racial discrimination in the athletic program. Consequently, Tiny reordered her priorities, focusing on music industry courses available at the college. Although the program offered many "great things," the general education curriculum and prescribed course sequencing discouraged her. Tiny described her experiences through the lens of race:

> When I first came to this school, the first two years I feel like I didn't learn nothing, like as a black person, you don't make it past your second year, so I felt like, you really get the most knowledge in college, your junior or senior year, because you can't take certain classes, unless you take prerequisites. You understand, "Oh, you can't take music 200, unless you take 100," or something. Why is it like that? I feel like those are the classes you really need. For instance, when I learned about one sheets. Why, people at home don't know what the hell a one sheet is, you understand what I'm saying? People that's dying to be rappers. They don't know you could simply go on the computer and do this little profile thing where it would tell you how to get your music played on the radio and we don't know this, at all. It's like something I would never search, one sheet. And I feel like it took me a long time to figure it out that I learned so much my junior and senior year in college. I didn't really learn nothing my first two years. I learned the same thing I really learned all over and over. The same stuff. English. The same thing. It helped me but, for the most part, I didn't learn anything that advanced my music, what I came here for, until my last two years.

Although the college offered many contemporary music classes, Tiny was upset by the absence of hip-hop and other forms of music in the curriculum:

> Nothing for us; no hip hop band, no R&B band. I feel like it's all classical, jazz, pop, funk. What about stuff that, what about reggae? What about soca? How you gonna call yourself a music industry program and y'all don't even . . . ya'll music is not that diverse. It might sound diverse. It might sound good, the audio classes and stuff but when it comes to really doing something I like, I love soca music, I love African music, I love reggae, I love hip hop, I love R&B. don't get me wrong, I love pop, funk, rock, I love all that too but I'm just saying, I wish I could take a class that was like Intro to Soca music, Intro to Reggae Music, Intro to Bob Marley or something [laughs].

Nonetheless, Tiny pieced together bits from course offerings that supported her aspirations, audio production techniques, social media marketing tips, intellectual property guidelines, tour budgeting models, and songwriting workshops. Even the courses that served her aspirations lacked substantial consideration of hip-hop or of the other types of music Tiny craved. She described her experiences in a songwriting course:

> When I first took songwriting. The professor looked at me like "This is songwriting class, okay?" before we did anything, mind you. You would expect he had some little bit of knowledge in rap music, just, I think I helped him out this year. I'm in there, I go up, I do my rap, he's like, "I'm going to be honest with you. I don't know nothing about rap." He couldn't even give me feedback at first. I need a teacher.

Andy Krikun

> I pretty much knew at 15 that I wanted to be a professional musician. There was just nothing else that entered my mind as a possibility of what to do with the rest of my life.

Andrew Krikun is a singer/songwriter, rocker, and educator whose musical experiences took him through the club scenes in Boston, Los Angeles, and New York, to graduate school, and later to teaching rock ensembles and songwriting at a community college. Andy was born in Brooklyn, New York in 1955, and moved to Northern New Jersey when he was 5 years old. As a child, Andy became interested in music and spent a great deal of time listening to music of various genres on the radio and on the family phonograph. As Andy's love for music grew, he was presented with opportunities at his school to learn to play an instrument. Andy recalled, "I had some failed attempts trying to learn violin at school and that didn't work out. After that, I tried clarinet in school, but then I got braces." Around the same time, Andy began to take private piano and immediately found a connection with his teacher based on the repertoire of the lessons. "I really liked my first teacher because it was kind of concurrent with my discovery of the Beatles, and he was willing to teach me Beatles' songs and still work on some traditional repertoire." Fearing that learning Beatles music was not 'serious enough' for private lessons, Andy's dad fired the piano teacher and sought to find Andy a teacher who would provide him with a more traditional approach to piano lessons.

Andy recalled that with the more traditional piano teacher, he quickly lost interest in piano lessons. "I was a rabid pop fan and remember coming home from school every day to listen to the countdown on the radio. I was into everything: Motown, pop, the Beatles, just everything that was out at the time." As Andy started to seriously listen to music again, he was exposed to the burgeoning folk music scene in New York City, and that spawned an interest in the music of Bob Dylan and Phil Ochs. Later, his knowledge of rock music expanded as he also listened to rock groups such as Creedence Clearwater Revival and Sly and the Family Stone.

Andy recalls having an epiphany in 1970, on the day that Jimi Hendrix died.

> I was infatuated with music at the time and I was crushed because I had gotten into music and just couldn't believe that he died. I had an epiphany that the football team wasn't really on my wavelength about it so that was the beginning of the end of my sports career.

At the age of 16, Andy's mother passed away after battling cancer and Andy remembers being alone a lot. It was during these alone times that he picked up the guitar and started to learn how to play. As Andy played around on the guitar, he found that his brief time taking piano lessons when he was younger provided a basis for him in his efforts to learn the guitar. Even after five years away from playing music of any sort, Andy remembered basic chords and chord structures and transferred that knowledge to the guitar. "I would learn everything from the Beatles to Dylan on the piano and guitar. I started playing their songs and writing my own at that point. That was the beginning for me."

Reflecting on first learning the guitar, Andy recalled that there was little connection between the music that he was interested in playing and the music ensembles at his school.

> I had nothing to do with any formal music program, school music or private lessons after the age of 11. I sort of prided myself on this idea of being self-taught and I wanted to follow the way that I thought my heroes had learned music, being self-taught.

Andy recalled using method books from Pete Seeger and Jerry Silverman, as well as listening to records and the radio to learn songs. Andy's dedication to learning the guitar soon led to music gigs around town. "I would perform at different events. You know, they would ask me to play my songs at libraries and talent shows." Andy recalled that one high school music teacher reached out to him and invited him to play a song in the school's annual holiday concert, even though Andy wasn't a member of any school music ensembles. Andy recalled being

> honored that he reached out and included me. Even though I personally rejected what was going on in school music, [he] recognized what I was doing and that I was involved in music outside of school, and that really meant something to me.

Playing in Bands

As Andy finished high school, he became more involved with music and playing out at various venues. "At that time I was really into the folk scene and I wanted to write and perform original stuff a la Bob Dylan and people that I admired. So I started to go to open mics in the city." Andy recalled that at that time, there were no opportunities in New Jersey to perform at an open mic night, so he would often travel to New York City, predominately to Gerde's Folk City in Greenwich Village to perform his music during open mic nights. Closer to home in New Jersey, Andy recalled a lack of performance opportunities because "the only gigs at restaurants were for people playing James Taylor and Cat Stevens songs."

Upon graduating from high school, Andy attended Boston University as a liberal arts major with the goal of studying philosophy and poetry while continuing to write songs. Andy also applied to Berklee College of Music in Boston, but as Andy put it, "I didn't think that Berklee was someplace where my idols, Bob Dylan or John Lennon, would have gone."

Andy recalled,

> I spent time in Boston and got in to R & B and blues and reggae and learned a lot through other musicians and fans—like I knew these Jamaican people in Boston and they turned me on to a bunch of stuff.

The diversity of musical influences played a large role in Andy's development as a musician. Andy explained, "I think the learning is about always being captivated by different types of music, and whether it was reading or getting the social and cultural context, it was a process of always listening and learning through a holistic process."

When Andy's Boston duo proved unsuccessful, Andy moved out to Los Angeles, California in 1978 at the age of 23 to pursue a music career full-time. Andy credits his move across the country as a catalyst for change.

> It wasn't until moving to Los Angeles that things really clicked and I was able to find the inner determination to make a serious go at it. L.A. was a place that you could reinvent yourself and things just clicked.

Los Angeles also provided a plethora of new musical influences that inspired Andy.

> Wherever I was, I was soaking up the energy of that place, but I hadn't been to a place like L.A. You had these incredible casts of characters and these different identities and you are trying to figure out where you fit. People talk about the rock and pop scene in L.A., but L.A. was and is like a smorgasbord of influences from reggae, African, punk, Mexican music and everything in between. I just never said, "I'm going to be a country singer or a rock musician." It was like taking the smorgasbord and combining those interests in order to see who I was as a musician.

Andy and the Rattlesnakes

Andy had the idea for his band before he started looking for musicians. He explained, "I'm not sure how I came up with the name but I always liked groups with a first name and band such as Rosie and the Originals,

Freddy and the Dreamers, etc." Andy was drawn to the 'rattlesnake' idea in an attempt to create a Southwestern identity separate from his New Jersey identity. Andy took several odd jobs, including working at a music store in Santa Monica called Platterpuss Records. It was at the record store where he met many of the musicians that would become part of Andy and the Rattlesnakes. The band started as a duo, then a trio, then a quartet, and then varied in size from 4–8 musicians. The most cohesive band consisted of six musicians in 1980–81. Andy started playing acoustic guitar with the band but was influenced to play the electric guitar by New York City bands such as the Talking Heads, Television, and the Patti Smith Group, as well as British groups such as the Clash.

Education

After graduating with a bachelor's degree in music from Hunger College in 1984, Andy returned to Los Angeles, where one of his odd jobs included working as a data entry and lab technician at a hospital. During his time at the hospital, Andy became good friends with a chemist from Nepal. Through this friendship, Andy became fascinated by the music and culture of Nepal and ended up spending time learning the music of Nepal with the Nepalese community in Los Angeles. Andy eventually traveled to Nepal and his experiences with world music led him to pursue a degree in ethnomusicology from UCLA.

While attending UCLA, Andy continued to be involved the band scene in Los Angeles, performing with the bands Urban Artillery and Blazing Wheel. He finished his master's program with a plan to move to Nepal and do field work for his PhD. After the birth of his daughter, however, the idea of taking her as an infant to Nepal for two years to do field work was not appealing to Andy. Instead, he moved back to the East Coast and took a job in the internet programming and web development industry. Although not initially interested in teaching, Andy took a job as an instructor of web programming at Westchester Community College and discovered that he enjoyed teaching. Andy soon began teaching music appreciation and music history, which led to his full-time job at Bergen Community College. At Bergen, Andy started the school's first popular music ensemble and songwriting class.

Conclusion

Andy still plays music, and joined with the original members of Andy and the Rattlesnakes to record some new material and play a reunion concert in Los Angeles in 2012. As he reflects now on his musical development, Andy hearkens back to the influence that his first piano teacher (who taught him Beatles songs) had on Andy's journey.

> My musical experiences inside of school were very separate from what I did outside of school. There was very, very little transference from what I learned in K–12 music and what I was doing musically, with the exception of that piano teacher early on who taught me about chords. In a way that might have been life changing because it gave me the tools to do what I wanted to do.

Andy's focus now is to facilitate musical experiences for his students so that he might have that same kind of impact.

> It's really about "Why would someone want to play?" It is like sparking that love, like a kid playing a riff. We all start the same way; learning the riff to Stairway to Heaven or Smoke on the Water, everybody starts there. Why do some people stop and why do some people keep going? That is the key. If we want students to find their love for music, we need to find the answer to that question.

DeVeor Rainey

DeVeor Rainey is a music educator, musician, and composer. Born in 1966 in the South Bronx borough of New York City, DeVeor's musical learning journey has taken her from listening to the radio as a little girl, through the birth of hip-hop, to teaching music in an East Harlem public school.

DeVeor's Childhood

DeVeor was born in 1966, and as she puts it "music was the thing that we had." Growing up without a television, the radio played an important role for DeVeor as both a source of entertainment and a source of information and new experiences. As a young girl, one of DeVeor's first musical memories was cleaning the house each Saturday. She described this task as an all day process, and while they cleaned, DeVeor's mother would blast the music on the radio. DeVeor recalled, "at that time we were dealing with doo-wop, and soul music, and funk music, and gospel music, and I was exposed to all genres of music." These experiences listening to the radio as a little girl provided a sense of joy to DeVeor and through these experiences, DeVeor built an emotional attachment to the music. "For me, it was it was a source of joy. And that stays with me to this day when I hear that music, it brings me a sense of joy."

School Music Education

DeVeor attended elementary school at the Harriet Tubman School in Harlem, where she recalled that her music teacher was an African American percussionist. "I remember he used percussion instruments to teach us music, and I remember learning St. Thomas by Sonny Rollins as one of the first pieces that I ever learned." DeVeor's elementary school also had vocal music, but DeVeor found herself intimidated by the process of singing out loud in front of others. The repertoire of the music program was a reflection of Harlem in the early 1970s. DeVeor recalled, "We learned freedom songs, because we were children coming out of the civil rights movement. We benefited directly from the civil rights acts and all of those acts of resistance. We learned spirituals, jazz, and the blues."

In junior high school, DeVeor attended a performing arts school, but didn't participate in any school music programs. "First, I went to dance, because I was following my friends, and then the second year, I went to drama." DeVeor recalled that the she didn't participate in the school music ensembles because the band and choir program were structured like traditional school music programs. DeVeor explained, "The vocal music program looked like your standard choir and the instrumental music program was your standard band program, and that experience looked very different from the music education experience that I had in elementary school."

In high school, DeVeor chose not to participate with school music ensembles because, as she described, "In high school I was a truant. I didn't do any music in high school because I wasn't into anything involved with school." The beginning of DeVeor's high school career also coincided with the emergence of hip-hop. Growing up in the epicenter of the hip-hop movement also changed how DeVeor felt about participating in school music ensembles. She explained,

> Honestly, even if there was good music programs in school, I wouldn't have been involved because my high school years coincided with the start of hip-hop and hip-hop didn't stress playing instruments, so I didn't bother with playing music in school.

For DeVeor, the emergence of hip-hop, and rap music specifically, spoke to her in a way that school music ensembles could not. She recalled:

> I was really into hip hop. I was there—I mean I wasn't a B-girl or a DJ or anything, but that music, that musical experience and the listening and the dancing, it was new and a vehicle for young people to express their experiences. That is where the focus was, and we weren't dealing with instruments.

Despite her self-described issues as a truant, DeVeor graduated high school and attended City College in New York City. In college, DeVeor didn't participate in music. "I majored in English, and I wasn't really doing much musically. The only constant was my listening experience and being exposed to different genres of music."

Music Learning in Adulthood

DeVeor's love and passion for music was rekindled once she had children. She explained,

> I got back into music when I was looking for a music program for my kids so that they would be, you know, well rounded people. So I took them to the Bloomingdale House of Music, which is a non-profit, community-based music program.

Initially, DeVeor planned to sign her children up for piano lessons, but when she arrived at the school there were not any available piano lesson slots, but there was space in an African percussion workshop. The instructor of the class was David Pleasant, a native of the South Carolina/Georgia Sea Islands. DeVeor recalled, "He was really into Gullah/Geechee music and body percussion, and I never used body percussion the way that he did. And he also used pitched percussion instruments, in the Gullah/Geechee tradition." DeVeor decided to sit in on the workshop and observe. She recalled that in the first class, "He would hand me a cowbell, and then the next week he would hand me something else. And I enjoyed playing with the group, so the next semester I enrolled in the class." DeVeor credits David Pleasant's African percussion class as "the beginning of me getting back into music and the source of my music training." In reflecting back on the musical relationship that she had with the ensemble, DeVeor views David Pleasant as more than just a music teacher.

> He became my mentor, he became my mentor. And that is why I use so many percussion instruments in my teaching. It is interesting to reflect back on the experiences I had in music class in elementary school, and the gap in time until I found this musical mentor who reintroduced me to music through percussion.

As DeVeor reflects on her life now as a musician, teacher, composer, she pays special attention to her role as a grandmother who is exposing her young granddaughter to music. She states,

> I think that we are innately musical, or have the ability to be musical. I think it is up to us as parents and grandparents to create enjoyable musical experiences for our children so that they have an emotional attachment to music.

Perspectives on Music Learning

In describing her history as a music learner, DeVeor explains, "I learned music from informal environments. My progressive understanding of learning happened when I became a parent. I was taught traditionally. My musical learning happened mostly from listening. My training, happened as an adult." DeVeor credits her children as the impetus for her participation in music as an adult. "I wanted my children to have musical experiences, so I kind of got back into music." As DeVeor reflected on her history music history, she shared that she wishes that she would have been more involved with school music programs in middle and high school, because she "would probably be a better musician, but I was following my peers and those school music programs didn't appeal to us. Most of the girls went to dance, so I went to dance."

She also shared her frustration about not being able to join band as an older student. She stated, "I thought about joining the instrumental music program my senior year, but they weren't going to let me into the instrumental program then, it is something you had to get into earlier."

DeVeor's case is unique in that she had very positive musical experiences as a young child, and then didn't participate in music making of any sort until adulthood. As she explained, "My musicality was dormant. I was a late bloomer. I mean, what opportunities are given to people who are really born to be musicians, but they don't come to that realization until later in life?" DeVeor also commented that narrow notions of music making and music experience fail to grasp the plethora of music making experiences that are happening everywhere. "When we see the bucket players on the street or the kids drumming on the tables, that should be viewed as a music education experience. They shouldn't be devalued. That should be significant, you know?"

Sean McPherson

Sean McPherson is a music educator and the co-founder and bassist of the Twin Cities hip-hop group Heiruspecs. In addition to numerous national headlining tours, Heiruspecs has opened for Cake, Ja Rule, Lyrics Born, The White Stripes, and many others. Additionally, Heiruspecs' music has been featured on Diddy's *Making His Band* and VH1's *Behind the Music*. Sean also serves as the Assistant Coordinator of the Hip-hop Studies program at McNally Smith College of Music in St. Paul, MN.

Sean McPherson grew up with a mix of in school and outside of school music education experiences. He spent the early part of his childhood in rural Massachusetts where he began playing rock guitar and bass through the influence of his older brother, whom Sean described as an "insufferable blues purist." Although Sean took a few private lessons on the guitar before middle school, the primary source of his music education began in the 7th grade when he began playing regularly with a friend who played the drums. In addition to playing together and giving each other lessons, they started playing with older musicians who were in their twenties and had some career experience.

As a teenager, Sean moved from Massachusetts to St. Paul, Minnesota and "fell in really quickly with a burgeoning hip-hop scene with a lot of guys who later made it nationally." Sean cited some key mentor–mentee relationships with older, more experienced musicians in the area as being a key element of his music education. McPherson soon began learning from Sean Hurley, who played bass for John Mayer as well as the band Vertical Horizon. McPherson described Hurley as "definitely the most pragmatically influential bass mentor that I had." McPherson credits much of his growth as a musician to the fact that he was able to learn the ropes from more veteran musicians.

Inside of School Education

During his high school years, Sean became involved with a digital recording program led by "this old jazz drummer," and that experience taught Sean that "you can have a musical experience inside of school that mimics a lot of the learning that goes on outside of school." The recording program at the high school focused on the development of musical artists. Sean recalled that the instructor:

> Didn't give me bass lessons, but he taught me tons about feel and musical applications, and he taught me tons about life skills about how much I should get paid, or teaching me that if I did my own promotions I

could ask for my own money other than being just a backup band. So it was a combination of some inspiration and career assessment that happened in that program.

Despite the strong connection that the high school recording program had with the students, Sean recollected, "there was this big schism between the upstairs band and choral program and the downstairs recording studio program. And basically you had to choose a side." This schism was largely a result in approaches to music education. While the recording studio focused on composition, recording, and pragmatic theory lessons, the upstairs jazz band was focused on getting the students' playing styles to mimic the great jazz musicians. Sean recalled:

I remember at the time, the jazz band director said, "If Count Basie were to come in here he would be embarrassed by how you're swinging," and I remember thinking, "If Count Basie came in here he would be ashamed that we were still playing things exactly the same way".

In contrast to the jazz band, the digital studio was free from the typical restraints of traditional music ensembles, including accepted canons repertoire, playing styles, etc. Students instead were encouraged to explore music that was meaningful to them and to book their own concerts in lieu of the traditional spring concert at the end of the year. Sean described his experience in the digital recording class as "much less teacher directed and much more lab-based."

The dichotomy between the focus of traditional in-school musical ensembles contrasted with the skills need to make it in the real world is problematic for McPherson. Sean referenced some jazz workshops that he attended as a student and compared the realities of learning the ropes of hip-hop performance to the safe boundaries of these jazz camps. Sean explained:

I did take a handful of jazz workshops growing up. In these workshops teachers had a responsibility to the campers and the parents to provide a safe and supportive environment for students to learn in. No such controls surrounded the informal education I experienced as an aspiring hip-hop performer. If you were weak you didn't get to rap again. If your set was bad you got cut off early and they didn't have you back. These harsh experiences had a much stronger impact on my improvement than the kid-gloves support of educators who are also aiming to please a paying mom in addition to teaching jazz.

(McPherson, 2012)

Outside of School Music Learning

As Sean graduated from high school, he spent a lot of time playing gigs at talent shows and open mic nights. Sean recalled that rappers performing to electronic beats primarily dominated the hip-hop scene in Minneapolis at that time. He explained, "With the prevalence of drum machines in hip-hop at that time, there weren't a lot of hip-hop shows where bands playing hip-hop using live instruments" (McPherson, 2012).

As McPherson began gigging more as a hip-hop bassist, he engaged in a lot of what he described as "informal learning practices." Sean defined informal learning practices as "the acquisition of knowledge from a source other than a person officially labeled a teacher" (McPherson, 2012). Sean explained that the knowledge gained from informal teaching practices could come from trial and error, the response of a crowd, or advice from an experienced person who educates as a mentor.

Sean also used the phrase "learning on the bandstand" to describe his real-world music education experience. He explained that to learn on the bandstand was efficient because "it doesn't willfully ignore the skills that might be most germane to a career in hip-hop such as the ability to rap on beat, interact with a crowd and prepare music that is mixed properly for stage performance" (McPherson, 2012). Compared to the static demands of the common music conservatory recital, McPherson believes that learning on the bandstand prioritizes the skills that are necessary for a performer.

Inside vs. Outside Music Learning Experiences

Another difference for Sean between music education in school and outside of school is that music education has the advantage of being able to divorce composition from competency. Sean stated, "As hip-hop is currently practiced we do not have this luxury. One can be a competent jazz musician without having ever written a bar of jazz music. By and large this is not the case in hip-hop" (McPherson, 2012). Sean further explained that if a new artist were to try and make their way in the hip-hop scene by just duplicating the raps of others who came before and they never wrote their own lyrics, they would not be taken seriously. Within the hip-hop community, the ability to write original lyrics and draw upon personal experiences for these compositions are signifiers of authenticity.

A key element of Sean's music education both inside and outside of schooling contexts came in the form of musical mentorship. In multiple cases, Sean learned from musical mentors. From bassist Sean Hurley to the jazz drummer that taught the digital recording class at McPherson's high school, Sean developed both his musical chops and his music business acumen through the tutelage of musical mentors.

Another aspect of Sean's musical development was the dichotomy between participation in school music ensembles and the real-world music education that he derived from a variety of places, including the digital audio class, performing gigs, and other informal learning opportunities. McPherson stressed the importance of real world experiences being as important as the development of his musical technique. Sean cited the artist development aspect of the digital recording class as more influential than the ensemble performance aspect of the jazz band class he took in school. The digital ensemble's focus on artist development, promotions, booking gigs, and performance contracts were much more useful to Sean as a developing artist than the traditional ensemble's focus on uniformity and group cohesion.

Implications for McPherson as an Educator

As Sean sought to teach hip-hop classes at McNally Smith College of Music, he approached hip-hop studies with a 'practitioner's reluctance'. Bringing into a college setting a style and approach to music that Sean learned informally through playing gigs and learning on the bandstand was problematic for McPherson. He explained that while he valued the informality of his hip-hop education, he believes he could have been better prepared for a career as a hip-hop artist if his formal education offered curriculum that considered the career demands of a professional outside of the academy (McPherson, 2012). Additionally, Sean believes that students who receive training inside the classroom will not have the respect in the hip-hop community that learning the same things outside of the academy would provide.

Shana Falana

Shana Falana is a singer, songwriter, and performer living in New York's Hudson Valley. She leads a band that bears her name, Shana Falana, a project Shana's pursued for over a decade. She records, tours, and promotes that project as her life's primary pursuit, one that "entails a lot of different things, technically, spiritually, emotionally, and musically." Shana's music falls into "four distinct genres." Those include "straight up silly pop music," "dream pop," "ethereal, non-lyrical but vocal driven, spiritual music," and "psychedelic, shoegaze rock."

Shana speaks about her work in ways that reveal three primary modes of music learning: private learning, oppositional learning, and social learning. All three modes share an experimental ethos, a pointed desire for musical experiences that "would totally set [her] imagination free."

For Shana, private learning dates back to her earliest memories, to when she was "like 6 or 7 years old" growing up in the San Francisco Bay area. Shana identified growing up around musical parents as primary influences. Her mother was a singer and songwriter. Early on, Shana "avoided becoming a musician" herself but privately took in the music of her mom, of her mom's record collection, and the popular music of the day. Shana explained:

> My mom was a singer and a songwriter so I grew up around music. There were a few records in the house that I loved. So I grew up appreciating music. I also had talent. I was just a talented girl and I could sing and I remember I had an *Annie* soundtrack, for whatever reasons, I would put that record on and I would sing to *Annie*, to other musicals, and I would sing to *Westside Story* and, you know, I would dance and I would perform and when my mother would be at work and I'd use my family's video camera [chuckling], I would videotape myself dancing and singing and I was just, I think I was born with a creative spirit.

Shana had similar experiences visiting her father on weekends:

> I remember being really, really young, seven, and my father was a jazz fan. He loved jazz music. My father didn't play but he would take me record shopping every weekend. I could pick out whatever I wanted. So, you know, as I started picking these things out, I would go home and I would listen. I became very emotionally connected to music at a very early age.

Much of this learning was "in private where I would just mimic what I was hearing, picking the notes out by ear. I always had a good ear so I could pick the notes out and learn what I wanted." In fact, Shanna "made a conscious decision not to become a musician" as a way of standing apart from her parents.

In that vein, Shana repeatedly described herself as "very defiant when I was a kid." That quality seemed to encourage another mode of music learning, oppositional learning, or learning marked by Shana's "conscious decision" to set herself apart. Many of her recollections reflect an oppositional response to the established ways of doing things, at least in the realm of music. Shana recalled, "even though my mother was, maybe because she was a singer and songwriter, I was convinced that I wouldn't do music, wouldn't ever be a musician, because I wanted to do something that was my own." Nonetheless, Shana, continued to explore and experiment with music by listening to records, learning by ear, and, for a short while, taking piano lessons with a private instructor. Shana's recollection of those lessons epitomizes the way in which oppositional learning informed her musical development. She recalled:

> I took piano lessons when I was a little girl, maybe around 7. That was the last time I tried to read sheet music. I remember my piano teacher, I would learn the song but I would make changes to it. I would rewrite some of the material and my teacher, well, let's say my teacher really frowned upon that [chuckles]. So I stopped taking piano lessons because I felt like it wasn't fun.

Even in private learning moments, Shana would mimic songs to a degree before "deciding, I didn't really want to learn it exactly like it was." Instead, she preferred to capture "the vibe or the essence of whatever it was that I was playing" and make it her own.

Those tendencies, to seek her 'own path' in relation to music she studied, remained constant throughout her childhood and adolescence. At the age of 17, Shana found herself living far from home, alone in the state of Montana. She sought out musical experiences as a way to cope, but again, very much on her own terms. Shana recalled singing

> a cappella in a bar. I sang like the Indigo Girls songs [chuckling], a cappella [chuckling], and people approached me and they were like, "oh you should be in our band." So that was how I got started. I was in Montana. I was on my own. Unexpectedly, I started performing and singing and songwriting.

Those first experiences in Montana represented some of Shana's first socially interactive music making, working with other musicians, as part of a local scene, networking, making connections, and building her skills, repertoire knowledge, and writing abilities along the way. Those new competencies served Shana well when she returned to her home town's then burgeoning music scene. Shana fondly remembered that period of her musical development:

> In the '90s in San Francisco, there was so much creativity. Everybody was sort of exploring, experimenting, and we were all supporting each other and it was just a great time to, to play with other people and to experiment with different sounds. So, that's what I did. I just explored all these different bands. Some of them I played guitar in. Some of them I played drums. Sometimes I'd just sing.

Two experiences during this period proved particularly influential on Shana becoming the individual musician she is today. The first experience was with a group of women, all musicians, singers, writers, and creative artists in their own right, and another as part of a regionally well-known band, The Gun and Doll Show.

During the 1990s, Shana met up with a group of San Francisco women to explore Bulgarian folk music, which was in the midst of a brief window of crossover notoriety in the US. Shana first heard the music on a recording from the English singer, Kate Bush, "I heard those sounds, the dissonance, the harmonies, I always had an ear for harmonies so I was drawn to it." The group turned out to be more than a singing or study group. It evolved into a creative community of practice, one in which Shana felt particularly free to explore new possibilities. She explained, in wistful and inspired tones:

> One glaring example [of music learning] in my head is definitely the women's Bulgarian group. It was just me and my friends getting together, a bunch of women in a dance studio with reverb from the echoing walls. We would experiment with improvising. I would play guitar or somebody would beat a drum and then we would read off of whatever words were available, like off a water bottle [chuckling], whatever words were around. We would sing the words and make up songs on the spot. It was always real tense moment because [laughing] because none of us knew what was gonna come out, you know that ugly duckling phase, but we would do it. That was probably one of the biggest teachers for me, that group, because we trusted each other enough to open up. It was really a big opening for me. I wrote a lot too, for that group. I would take songs, like the Bulgarian songs, and I would write piano parts and then we would rework it so I would sing like a traditional song and then I would write something for it, like a guitar part. I

would even rewrite some of the melody, *exactly* what I was told not to do when I was 7 [laughing].

Outside of the Bulgarian folk group and various other bands, Shana found herself part of The Gun and Doll Show, a Bay area band that was quickly gaining recognition and on the verge of being signed to a record label. Although Shana recalled her experiences in that group as "a really great time," tensions with the band's leader made her more resolute to pursue her own path.

Not unlike her private reworking of material she learned by ear as a child or her determination to rearrange the piano repertoire assigned by her teacher, Shana found herself uneasy playing parts dictated to her by the band's leader. At one point, Shana recalled the leader telling her, "You're not a songwriter. You're someone who should sing other people's songs, like Billy Holiday." Shana deeply disagreed in a way that marked a turning point: "I'll never forget it. I knew he was wrong because I had written music my whole life. I ended up leaving that band right as they were about to be signed." Shana left San Francisco for Brooklyn, New York where she established a new life working her way into a new music scene, new contacts, new opportunities, and new challenges.

In New York, Shana pursued music, but for its own merits rather than as a career. Certainly, music was her career, but the experiences from her childhood, from Montana, and from the Bay Area music scene of the '90s cemented her view that music was "something more, something spiritual, a way to make [her] own path." Upon leaving the difficult situation in San Francisco, Shana vowed:

> I swore then, I would never pursue music as a career. I felt like music was sacred. I really fell into it and felt like it was this really powerful, sort of sacred medium and that it, it needs to be preserved and it should never have money attached to it. I remember having that thought distinctly.

Neville Peter

Neville Peter was born in 1972 in St. Thomas, a US Virgin Island. He is a gospel musician who today dedicates his musical energy to his deep spiritual convictions. His music education journey brought him from his first teacher, the radio, out from under the piano in the small churches on his Caribbean island town through the University of Miami's prestigious Jazz Music program, to the recording studios and live stages of award-winning recording artists in various genres, and now back to the churches that resemble those he grew up in.

Born with glaucoma, his vision deteriorated to blindness by the age of 12. Despite this impairment, he has developed into an incredible musician whose musical fluency is a reflection of his diverse experiences both 'inside' and 'outside' institutions of music education. His musicianship began to emerge by age 5 where he first started singing publicly in church. He was teased by his young friends for singing and consequently "toned it down." Neville did, however, receive some encouragement from more senior members of the congregation who asked, "why didn't I hear you this Sunday?" This emotional tug of war between his peers teasing him and the elders encouraging him wore on Neville, eventually distancing him from making music. Although he took several years off from singing publicly, his musical talents ultimately needed an outlet.

At the age of 14, Neville began studying piano as an elective at school. This 'inside' musical activity eventually allowed him to "rediscover his voice at a high school Christmas concert where he received a standing ovation." Shortly thereafter he began receiving invitations to sing at other concerts, church events, and talent shows on the island. The encouragement and positive feedback led him to pursue his personal musical interests in jazz, pop, reggae, and R&B. While in high school, he often gigged at local nightclubs, but "out of respect for [his] parents, still attended church and would sing there from time to time."

When he was 19, Neville left St. Thomas and moved to Miami, FL, where he attended the University of Miami on a full scholarship in the Studio Music and Vocal Jazz program. While there he received an award from *Downbeat Magazine* for best National College Jazz Male Vocalist of the Year. As he worked 'inside' on his theory, improvisation, and performance skills at the university in the daytime hours, he took what he learned 'outside' on nights and weekends performing and rethinking jazz, funk, R&B, and pop music in nightclubs on South Beach and around South Florida.

Outside of School Professionally

Neville's exposure and musical reputation earned him opportunities to tour 'outside' with Cassandra Wilson and Gladys Knight. It seemed Neville was poised for a fruitful career in popular music, but within a few years of graduation Neville experienced a spiritual revelation leading him to dedicate his musical efforts away from secular music. In Neville's own words, "God's divine providence" interceded. He resolved to give all his talents to God, withholding nothing. Since then, he has written hundreds of gospel songs and has had the privilege of sharing the stage with Bishop T. D. Jakes, Gladys Knight, Donnie McClurkin, Yolanda Adams, Natalie Cole, Shirley Caesar, Richard Smallwood, Kurt Carr, Bebe Winans, and many others. He has performed at the White House and at Carnegie Hall and has appeared on many television programs, including TBN's *Praise the Lord* program, *I-Gospel* with Alicia Williamson, *Celebration of Praise* with Ron Rosson, and *Cynthia and Friends*.

Neville's diverse musical education has richly informed who he is as a musician. His early experiences as a child in church singing and playing piano influenced his university jazz education, which in turn impacted his professional collaborations and real-world opportunities. This led him back to his commitment to return to his roots as a singer and pianist in spiritual music. It should be noted that it took a combination of 'inside' and 'outside' influences to bring him to where he is currently on his musical journey.

Reflections on Outside and Inside Learning

Neville was asked to reflect on his past musical learning experiences, and, in particular, to compare the nuances intrinsic to his 'inside' and 'outside' music learning experiences. Neville explains that at the university, "faculty frowned on that 'outside' stuff . . . it wasn't maybe as legitimate or real because it didn't have the analytical/educational aspect to it." Neville noted that he often argued with his professors on that issue, pointing to the fact that the very music being studied 'inside' arose 'outside' the walls of a university.

Neville expressed appreciation for both the 'inside' and 'outside' worlds. Without both, he might not have been able to cultivate a balanced musicianship.

> For me, improvisation didn't really come naturally in terms of playing piano. I needed the institutional education to help me understand what that was all about. As a singer, I really didn't need to be taught a lot, but as a pianist, I really needed the structure.

Neville points out that the structure unfortunately did inhibit his creativity and the artistic side of musicianship. "My teachers often made improvisation sound so restrictive, not encouraging me to think outside the box."

Speaking of 'outside' influence, Neville notes the radio as his primary influence.

> The radio was my best friend. I would sing along to all kinds of music. If anything was my teacher, it was that. There was something intuitive about listening and emulating what I heard. I'm a firm believer that experience is your best teacher.

But Neville is careful to clarify.

> I really needed college to help me understand some concepts that I kind of knew about before but never had formal constructs to define them. Once I learned the ideas again through a conceptual framework, it brought order to all the sounds I had going on in my head. For example, taking the jazz vocal arranging classes, singing those awesome arrangements in the jazz vocal ensembles, learning the classical theory and applying it really helped shape me. Now, decades after college I honestly can admit that I cannot remember the rules of music anymore. It's just assimilated and incorporated into what I do naturally and intuitively.

Into the Future

Neville admits that music learning is a lifelong experience.

> Now when I listen to music, I'm still learning. I constantly just tear things apart and listen over and over. After I figure whatever it is I'm listening to, I notice that it appears in my own expressive way in the music I'm making.

Neville explains that he no longer listens to music like he did when he was a student considering what extension was being used on a certain appealing or surprising chord.

> Now it's kind of like speaking English. We don't think about putting this verb after this noun. I honestly don't even think about the theory at all, and if I were to go back to school, I'd probably need a refresher course.

Time has not only distanced Neville from 'inside' curricula, it has also disconnected him from his associations with other musicians he once was close to at the university. He admits that now, 'outside' of the institution, he has done very little collaboration. He cited collaborations with some friends from college who now live thousands of miles away. They did some internet file swapping and recorded a few things together, but never did physically share the same space and collaborate on a project. "I didn't even get to meet some of the other players on the tracks we worked on." Neville also notes that his commitment to non-secular music may have distanced him from working more with people he used to work with when he was 'inside' the university.

Although Neville spends most of his musical time alone in his studio and performing solo acts in churches, he has adopted a few mentees—some local and some from across the globe.

> Generally, I try to mentor them and we figure out things together, like what makes melodies memorable and share back and forth. I've even given workshops all the way in Australia on songwriting; just trying to share all the principles I learned 'outside' school . . . things I haven't heard of any formal songwriting classes that teach that. I mean I didn't have that stuff when I was in college. The songwriting I learned wasn't from school. I learned from listening to the radio. I ask questions like why I like it and how might it appeal to other people. I don't really think that the training from college really is how I write my songs.

Spiritual and Untrained Connections

Ultimately Neville attributes most of his musical abilities to a higher power.

> I find it really amazing that there is this intuitive thing. First of all it's a God-given gift. I'm not trying to brag, nobody taught me to sing. It was just natural to me—almost like another language, and I have been speaking that language since I was about 5 years old. And I have witnessed it at churches, seeing little kids sitting under the piano watching everything . . . studying like that . . . I have seen that with drums too. I went to a church and this little 12-year-old was amazing! I mean he was a whole lot better than some of those kids from the university. Now I'm not sure, but I think that little drummer studied by watching. I'm not sure if he ever had a teacher telling him how to hold the sticks and teach him technically. I think it was intuitive. It happens to a lot of kids, I've seen it a lot. I have collaborated with such kids, and it's really weird, I didn't have to tell him anything. We didn't even discuss the music.

Neville notes that he has had interesting musical experiences collaborating with untrained musicians. He has jumped into a music collaboration with someone without being introduced or communicating with them verbally—instead only communicating with musical sounds. He's done this and found out afterwards that all along he was playing with a self-taught child who learned exclusively by listening. He remarked that he did that too.

> I was copying Bobby McFerrin when I was little. I still do that now. So boiling it down to where you can't reduce it anymore . . . some people are able to analyze music in ways that allow them to express intuitively and others need to have the analytical side to help them to . . . I have experienced both sides as a singer and a pianist.

Summary

In summary, Neville considers himself an instinctive musician who has a divine gift for singing, which was cultivated 'outside' through lots of imitation, listening, and singing in real-world settings such as nightclubs and churches. Although his 'inside', school-based education deepened his understanding of some music theory and piano playing, what he practices now is so assimilated into his thinking that he isn't analyzing as he once did 'inside' college. The cerebral processes of active listening, audiation, and systematically breaking down harmonies and melodies into their core components are all in the past for him. Now he uses music much like a fluent speaker constructs sentences out of nouns and verbs. It feels automatic to him. He attributes this to the combined 'inside' and 'outside' music educations he received and fostered for himself. Whereas the formal education he received 'inside' at the university was bound by four years of rigor and structure, those 'outside' music education experiences are ongoing and broad in scope.

Neville refers to a kind of musical detachment where he lets go of the analytical thought waves and just reacts to the music he plays with the tools, gifts, and instincts his previous musical learning experiences have instilled in him. He prepares for performances and writes music in a much freer manner now because of this fluency. Neville knows that music education in both 'inside' and 'outside' contexts was important for him and is available whenever possible to assist his mentees. Those mentees will likely be the beneficiaries of a diverse musical perspective that joins the 'inside' with the 'outside', adding to the diversity and richness of music education's possibilities for generations to come.

Raymond Wise

Raymond Wise is a fourth-generation church musician whose roots extend to his great-grandmother, who was a radio promoter of gospel music. He learned music in the context of family and home life. One of six children, he was born in the 'younger trio'. As Ray describes, the three siblings before him had already formed a musical group before he was born. He and his siblings grew up in a musically rich environment that nurtured a merging of music and life. The two were woven together in ways that Ray describes as "inseparable." In fact, Ray describes his musicianship developing prior to birth, where he can be 'seen' in family pictures still in his mother's womb as she and his siblings were "singing near a mic."

Under the tutelage of his first mentors, his mother and grandmother, Ray learned to play gospel-style piano. He learned through imitation, often connecting the sounds his grandmother valued and then promoted on the radio, which, in turn, Ray imitated and integrated into his piano playing style. By the time Ray was old enough to participate in organized music making, he found access through church children's choirs. But these choirs were far from musically childish. As Ray explains, there was little to no regard for "age appropriate music." Instead, little children were "praised and lauded for being able to imitate the musical sounds of adults." Ray, alongside his church peers, cultivated a strong voice in these contexts, developing musical skills such as part-singing, vibrato, and a general confident musical identity.

Ray explains that by the time he made his way to elementary public school, he already stood out as a musical leader because of the musical skills he had gained from church music. Early church music contexts, in many ways, were integral to Ray's fashioning of his identity as a musician. The safety of being surrounded by family and loved ones fostered a fertile nesting ground for his musical identity. From this sprang forth a confident young musician ripe for leadership in elementary public school.

Continued Learning

While in school, Ray demonstrated the attributes of a solid musician. He brought the sounds of the church to his school choir. He didn't do this alone, though. Many of his teachers in school were also leaders and elders in the church. Ironically, the music teachers at church didn't always teach music at school, and this led Ray to develop his musicianship in diverse contexts, where he was molded into a musician with varied skills/attributes.

Ray was surrounded by a vibrant community of gospel musicians who were always around him both inside and outside school. They came from places such as Peabody and Howard University and served as positive black role models who he aspired to be like. These students were church musicians who studied classical music in conservatory. As Ray described, these mentors could "do all of it."

Ray's continued growth and maturation existed within the context of music, but extended into social and spiritual spheres, which were cultivated through mentorship. In Ray's words, his mentors were "spiritual, musical, social and educational mentors who were not shy to correct children and get them to do things correctly." His public school life in the Baltimore/Washington, DC area was not necessarily the sort that you might conceive of as "traditional school music." Ray describes his school choirs as gospel choirs. By the time Ray was of age to move to university, many of his musical skills were not "honored by the institution of university music schools." Fortunately, he did have a variety of musical skills, but the ones that were mostly used in gospel music settings didn't seem to be valued by his teachers in the university. It is this missing link, between church music and school music, that Ray now works to bridge. He has dedicated his energies to promoting gospel music to people who want to learn the skills and craft associated with it.

Passing It On

For more than 30 years now, Ray has worked with the Center for Gospel Arts teaching people how to "do gospel music." With emphasis on organ, piano, composition, arranging, and singing, Ray has developed pedagogy and methodology to prepare teachers to promote and perpetuate the tradition of gospel music. Ray serves as a professional church musician and clinician who spreads his knowledge of gospel music in many environments in and out of school. Ray also is a professor at Indiana University, where he works to prepare music education majors to teach gospel music.

As Ray describes, "gospel music is done differently depending on contexts." It can be more educational in one setting and more inspiration in nature in another. The key to making it work in multiple contexts is that he has developed some methodology and pedagogy to teach it to all kinds of learners so that it is accessible. In order to do this, Ray describes himself as "having to know how to take the arts and adjust it so you can find a way to fit it in." Ray explains, "we have created an academic art form that can be assessed by those not from the background."

Ray's use of academic buzzwords such as 'assessment', 'adjudication', and 'methodology' reflects his understanding of the nuances associated with school-based institutionalized music teaching and learning. Ray bridges both the academic and spiritual/church worlds because he sees a demand and need for formalized approaches to learning gospel music. Ray explains, "people come from all backgrounds because they want to access the music in spite of their beliefs."

Ray notes that although the tradition of gospel music has been passed down through rote instruction, there are always ways to notate the music and make it possible for more traditional style musicians to integrate their musicianship into the experience. He regularly directs collegiate and professional choirs and orchestras whose eyes might be divided between sheet music and mimetic rote learning. Ray explains that these participants often become consumed with the emotional and spiritual outflow of energy from the music. Gospel music workshops become extra-musical experiences in which powerful emotions and community building are facilitated by the merging of learning and musical styles bridged through his use of standard notation, orchestra, choir, and well-conceived methods for instructing and passing on the gospel music tradition to those who are "not from the church."

Church-Style Learning

Ray describes that in the 'church style', many people use the "show me approach" where they learn a song by standing around and watching a master do it. He also describes a different approach where learners use a "figure it out approach" where learners imitate a sound to the point where they actually sound exactly like recordings. This normally happens though under the guidance of a mentor-type figure who will "invest time and energy in a mentee." In Ray's words,

> once a mentor discovers someone has some potential, they invest in them. And then you have a musician who plays very well, but who may have never stepped in an academic setting. They may play very well and have an ear that allows them to play anything, but they lack the standard notation reading skills promoted in institutional settings. Those musicians might end up without the ability to read. Even if they have private lessons, they may lean towards what they grew up in.

This is why Ray sees opportunity to take church style music learning out into non-church contexts and bring more traditional music learning approaches back to church musicians. He is working on cultivating both the 'written' and the 'aural' so they can move from one setting to another.

Ray speaks of a concern he has for the next generation of musicians to communicate with and learn from previous generation musicians. His fear is that they are not communicating much unless forced to do so. This is where he feels that the 'show me' approach might be most beneficial, allowing generations to share sounds, voicings, and stylings that can migrate back and forth through musicians regardless of age and background.

Summary

Ray Wise brings the outside in. He views music from a composer's standpoint, but brings it back to performers and educators looking for ways to perpetuate an ongoing musical sharing between peoples. He continues growing and adding to his musical tool kit, which he describes as "keeping you moving." Ray explains that gospel music has continued to evolve in five distinct areas, which he has documented in his scholarly writing, and he hopes to continue to promote it by taking it to the streets through a "sacred/ secular interchange."

Ray is well on his way to realizing this goal. His dedication is closely tied to the Center for the Gospel Arts, a community arts program that he runs. For over 28 years Ray has worked to curate, cultivate, and disseminate gospel music to people. His work with many children, starting early on in their lives, has led them to pursue their doctorates in music. As Ray describes, "many of my kids grow up alongside me in places like the Gospel Arts Summer Camp where a continual cycle of mentoring, writing of original songs, and making of CDs leads children to become great musicians."

Ray explains,

> my goal is . . . I know I will not do this forever, so I'll need to pass this on to the next generation. As music evolves and people look for formal ways to assess and train, we can identify those people with those skills and I'm really excited that I am helping make that list grow.

Ray is also looking to create an online school where people anywhere can access gospel music learning. This will make it practical for even more learners to cultivate their gospel music skills. Ray Wise is 'wise' because he knows exactly what people need to learn to be gospel musicians, and he is finding ways to codify and train it to people so they "get it on purpose and not just by accident."

Jean Baptiste Craipeau

Jean Baptiste (JB) Craipeau is a musical multi-selfer teetering the line between reality and virtuality. A musical multi-selfer is a person who digitally musics with themselves in both synchronous and asynchronous fashion. They record themselves in layers and make clones of themselves in asynchronous fashion, but then record alongside themselves in synchronous fashion. This is an iterative process that builds up the sound of a single self into a multi-self. I first met JB over ten years ago through a mutual curiosity in a cappella music in an asynchronous online discussion board. I found him because he was transcribing Take 6 arrangements. Take 6 is a world-renowned a cappella ensemble known for their graceful yet sophisticated vocal harmonies. Today, I found JB on YouTube posting videos of himself singing some of those multi-part arrangements. I also found him on YouTube performing with a virtual a cappella group called Accent. He describes them as six men in five different countries.

Mentoring and Online Culture

Evident on YouTube and other popular social media, musical multi-selves are significant components of the current popular and participatory musical landscape. JB collaborates with himself and finds ways, through technology, to build up his musical potentiality. He posts many videos on YouTube and receives communication from viewers asking for arrangements and tips. Through the online culture, JB acts as a mentor.

JB's mentors were situated in a variety of contexts, online and in person. Mainly, though, JB has great ears and attributes much of this to his experience transcribing Take 6 arrangements. He cultivated his musicianship through a lot of lonely personal time. Prior to technological innovation, JB, still in high school, would write transcriptions and then look for collaborators. While his father was a musician, choir director, and music lover, he still didn't have anyone to sing along with. His father did have the vinyl of Take 6 and many other greats. This was the catalyst for his collaboration with himself. JB found himself listening and transcribing. This was a rather lonely time looking around for musical collaborators, but there were none. "I came from a place of being alone. No one cared about this music so I just did it myself."

At first, JB just worked on audio on some crude tape-based multi-trackers. He realized quickly that there were others doing barbershop tags and sharing them. He quickly learned how to do this on the computer and started posting his ideas/recordings to YouTube. In the early days of YouTube, it was a small community. "I started forming a family there. People were sharing and caring about this kind of music." JB explains that this helped get him more precise in his recordings. "The whole world is watching . . . made more critical of my voice."

The mentoring community that he found himself in online was helpful. He exchanged emails with others like him, some at advanced levels with better equipment than his. This pushed him and led him to trying some more sophisticated recording techniques. One mentor suggested to him that not only was the audio important, but so was the video. Today JB makes fun and visually engaging multi-self videos. Check out his recording of "Let's Groove Tonight," which he recorded without a chart and exclusively by ear. This is an outgrowth of this advice.

Approximately four years ago, JB received communication from one of today's most well-known multi-selfers: Jacob Collier. Jacob was asking for help figuring out how to do some multi-selfing. "Jacob is amazing . . . he's better than me at everything. I feel very lucky to have that early connection with him. Today Jacob has friends like Quincy Jones." I asked JB if he considers himself Jacob's mentor. JB explains, "I don't know . . . but he was like hi JB do you know how to make the video editing happen."

Exploring Identities

JB describes himself as a bass player. He has learned to sing better with time. It is interesting to note that JB considers his singing poor on the bass parts. He has had to learn how to do vocal frying to get the low notes to come out. Vocal frying is a technique singers use to get a crackling low pitched sound out of their voice. This is not a common vocal technique used by conventional singers. Perhaps, and this is conjecture from the perspective of this author, JB enjoys making music in potentialities. He refuses to be bound by a single musical identity. For instance, is it a coincidence or intentional that JB posts videos of himself singing bass parts, yet identifies as a person who plays bass, yet feels he can't sing bass? Is it pure happenstance that JB writes arrangements for multi-part singing, but can't find collaborators in his local community to do it with him, and instead mediates much of this through some form of technology?

JB explains that he is an arranger, and an arranger is often lonely. "My approach is to be able to put my charts up to be visible by groups so they could adapt it to a live performance." Sadly, while people do perform his charts or adapt them, he rarely gets people to share with him what the final product sounds like. "So, yeah, being an arranger, it's lonely. The sounds are in your head like potential, imaginary things." To take things a step forward, JB likes to record his arrangements so he can hear them. "It's really different than a composer pre-technology writing on paper and imagining on their own in the candlelight."

Ironically, JB's musical style of choice is one that, traditionally at least, requires other singers. JB explains that at the heart of a cappella singing is community with other people. "It's your whole body working . . . not like playing bass and drums, it's more than that." When pressed for whether or not he experiences that same sensation when multi-selfing, he says,

> well, you're still alone in your room. There's still a feeling at some point in the process. I like to wake up at 7am and start recording until midnight and finish on day 4–5. I find some pure joy to try some stuff that works and I kind of get that feeling when in a group too.

Learning

I asked JB about his family life as a child and now as a dad. He explains that he "also believes in the environment." We laughed about how time is harder to come by with a family to care for. His five consecutive 17-hour days in the studio rarely happen now with his little baby in the house. He does expose his daughter to some things in the studio. "If your family is into sport, then they will go that way . . . same for music." His father and mother naturally gave him the ingredients to be musical and he's expecting similar things to happen for his daughter.

Perhaps JB learned so much of his precision and discipline in his conservatory experiences. JB attended a musical university in France and a conservatory. "I went to both things, learning double bass jazz and classical harmonies in both schools. Then I choose my way which is more popular and jazz with the strict skills wedded to the classical thing."

Mainly though, JB developed much of his musicianship through close listening. His ears developed through transcription and through the iterative process of recording himself in multi-self recordings.

Creative Process and Potential for Performing

JB describes his recording process as non-creative and systematic.

> Most of the time I have a midi track going to help keep the pitch and groove. I sing with that. If I'm feeling comfortable, I mute the midi and sing along with the vocals to match the pitch. This helps with intonations.

JB prefers to sing passages correctly rather than to go in and do micro edits on the computer. Same for pitch correction. "I prefer to just sing it right the first time."

When asked if he has performed live, he explains that he hasn't done any of his recordings live, although his mother has encouraged him. "I haven't figured out a way to do this live yet." He describes live loopers who do this as interesting, but truly not his thing.

> Live looping is cool for three songs but it gets boring after a while . . . here's the bass part ok dm dm dm . . . It could work with a four-chord song or four-song moments. It could be done with some backing tracks have every track playing except one you sing live, but I'm like, "why sing that?"

Some people have told JB, "wow you are amazing doing all this stuff without other people." "They tell me, it's like magic. And I'm like no, that's wrong, because for me I'd rather sing it live."

JB explains that inherent to the style of a cappella is a kind of musical stiffness trying to perfect and lock all the chords. "I could write new chords that don't even exist yet, like Jacob Collier . . . you let your finger go where they want and some nice movement, melody and chords could just be created (finger snap)."

Final Thoughts

A musical multi-selfer like JB is supposed to be a little lonely. They work with themselves and need the spaces and places to negotiate those choices and musical collaborative ideas with themselves. They are more than likely highly skilled and precise. This is a function of the alone time, the reflectivity inherent to the process and the technological tools that mediate the process in today's technologically driven musical environment. JB embodies many musical dualities. He is a bass player who sings, a learner who mentors, a writer who records, a musical purist who mediates through technology. He has serious musical conservatory training yet records covers and posts funny videos on YouTube. JB has the musical ears and skills that transcend time, yet he bridges traditions and practices through the leverage of the tools of synchronicity, asynchronicity, reality, and virtuality.

Truth Universal

Truth Universal, a native Trinidadian, and resident of New Orleans, grew up in a rich and diverse musical milieu. He most strongly identifies himself as a black American with African roots and many of his rhymes today are postured around social justice themes from a marginalized Afro perspective. In a recording entitled *Hands Off Assata*, he shares that he is, "Red, Black and Green in case you forgot," paying homage to Marcus Garvey and the UNIA (Universal Negro Improvement Association) movement. In his early years, he could not deny his environment. The blending of African, Caribbean, jazz, second line, soca, calypso, reggae, funk, and R&B yielded a contemporary musician who prides himself on preserving the early elements of hip-hop. His most recent music video, "Into the Future," was recorded on 8mm analog tape, honoring the traditions and rawness of the past while looking into the future.

Truth's early experiences learning the art and craft of hip-hop did not take place in school or institutions. Instead, Truth would go to the supermarket on weekends with his family and then sneak over to the record store where he first learned to "dig in the crates" for sample material. Truth's neighborhood buddies showed him how to make beats on the early versions of the Boss Dr. Rhythm and then scratch either his or his father's old records over the drum machine. Fortunately for Truth, he never got in trouble with his father for destroying records as he cultivated his hip-hop musicianship through youthful exuberance when he "first caught the bug." By following the lead of a few friends who first taught Truth the role of DJ and later how to MC, he found himself exposed to an ever-growing audience and listenership in his college years.

A Professional Is Born

Although he didn't have much in the way of access to technology such as recording studios, Truth began to make recordings whenever possible and eventually got those recordings in the hands of radio station DJs. Looking back, Truth admits it would have been a lot easier if he had hired a marketing team to help promote his music. Instead, Truth promoted his music at battle scenes where he and other rappers would fight each other through freestyling to establish themselves in front of audiences cheering them on. It was there that Truth found opportunity to sell his music and gain wider recognition.

Truth has strong ties to New Orleans, but prides himself on being "worldwide, getting love from everywhere." He would not be the first rapper to boast of his fame, but it is in this sense of pride and self-confidence that

Truth lives up to his name through his convictions. His songs are filled with bold declarations of categorical type opinions and perspectives with implications pointing to institutional racism, justice, and a pressing need for social change. Truth rap:

> You offended by the wording, well I do not care. Standing by my convictions as long as there's air . . . an emcee with the warrior flare affecting social change. Invent the future . . . main intent of my career.

Truth has shared the stage with Talib Kweli, dead prez, Mos Def, The Roots, Alanis Morrissette, Michael Franti, Immortal Technique, Luciano, and Zion. In spite of the pride he has for being a New Orleans staple in the Southern hip-hop scene, his broader collaborations with professionals is something Truth wants his listeners to know about.

Reflections on Learning

Truth did have some music education in his elementary schooling; however, as he transitioned to middle school, he did not know who to contact and how to make his way into the music classes. It was this pivotal moment where Truth disconnected from school music education and instead focused on learning on the outside. Truth's primary influences, the radio and TV, allowed Truth to know what was going on in NY and the East Coast where hip-hop was prominently evolving. Occasionally, people would bring fads down to New Orleans that Truth would assimilate into his sound and style. He refers to learning as a sort of 'osmosis' where learning was invisible and transmitted from person to person often unintentionally.

Truth thinks that hip-hop is something that one can do so long as they have the artistic flare. He admits that a hip-hop school might be able to provide students with some of the formal elements that students might be able to "learn and regurgitate," but "true artistry does not come from a blueprint where students with A's have any real skills." Truth learned best when he "studied and mastered the craft" which later allowed him opportunity to be "blessed to be on tour."

Truth is excited about the possibilities technology is affording young artists today. He sees great potential for students to "find mp3s and feed them to programs like Reason or Fruityloops." Young rappers today can express themselves by first sitting down and patiently learning how to use software. He admires the artistic potential this presents to the next generation. In his early days, as he was learning, it was a much more cumbersome process to make a beat. It was through this process that he developed an "ethic where he would only sample from records."

Preserving the past by looking to the future is what Truth does when he mentors young artists. He proudly shares his experiences with his mentees, who he feels are advancing their careers much faster than he did because he can give them career and artistic advice he never had.

Surviving Age

In one of Truth's songs, "Praise the Lord," he says, "it's safe to say I'm a product of the blocks I've explored," suggesting that Truth constructs his identity and sense of who others perceive him to be through life experiences. Truth goes on to say he "paid dues the average cat cannot afford," meaning the construction of self was not always an easy one.

Perhaps it was in Truth's experiences of learning how to rap and living the life that gave him ideas worth sharing in songs and rhymes that are all part of his outside school experience. The so-called school of hard knocks and street culture that define hip-hop culture are precisely the authentic learning scapes in which the musical style is harvested. The hardships of rappers' lives have been no secret to listeners, as these themes are pervasive in the lyrics of so many hip-hop songs. In Truth's case, he ties much of this identity to New Orleans: "New Orleans 9th ward working class section 8 destitute, but still contribute to the collection plate."

The New Orleans 9th ward was hit hard by Hurricane Katrina in 2005, resulting in a slow rebuilding process. From this disaster hatched a deep sense of survival in Truth. He shared his stories of losing everything, including his priceless records, which were warped by sunlight as they were drying after the storm out on the front porch. Through losing everything, the contagion of rebuilding continues to work in Truth as an aging rapper. Truth's songs are filled with survival themes such as "I'm a spit till kingdom comes, that's my best estimate . . . You intend to make me cease, you got trouble to bear."

In another of Truth's songs he shares, "I'm a fixture, I ain't going anywhere. Not falling off, I show improvement every year." Perhaps it is in between these words that one can see the vulnerability of an aging rapper who admitted in an interview, "I'm an old dude who's old for the game of hip hop." Truth embraces the younger generation and sees other aging rappers falling off because they want too badly to preserve the past and have consequently fanned the flames of the old–young divide. It is in this bridging of old school rap with the new that Truth hopes to remain relevant and continue to learn.

Summary

Truth Universal learned through life. His personal story is one of struggle, hardship, and caring enough about the experiences to share with the world. He knows who he is and wants desperately to share it with the world.

Through this sharing he constructs his own personal and musical identity. His identity is tied closely to his beloved New Orleans, a city rich with culture and people with diverse backgrounds. There he finds social acceptance through his Afro roots trickling down into his music. "Black business first, the difference my complexion makes."

Truth learned almost everything he raps about and how to do that rapping outside of the walls of institutions. His videos are almost always outdoors as well. He is an outside musician in a true sense of the word. His ideas regarding society and awareness of injustice coupled with his hip-hop skills are validated by his years on the scene and his prolific performing and recording experiences. In Truth's words: "It's my pleasure and my duty . . . my love laden chore . . . I put stock in my quotes." Truth keeps it real and keeps himself constantly moving forward. His story most certainly should inspire the next generation of rappers to learn their craft outside and be a source of Truth for the future.

Jay 'J-Zone' Mumford

Jay 'J-Zone' Mumford does "a little bit of everything" out of necessity, curiosity, and quickly shifting focus. "In order to make a living, to survive, to get by," he has had to learn bits and pieces of engineering, producing, drumming, rapping, and negotiating the music business in pursuit of his career in hip-hop. Jay works producing beats for hip-hop artists and for other performers. Recently, he has come to specialize in recording vintage style drum breaks, recorded on period drum kits.

Jay's life in music started in his native Westchester County, New York, a suburb just north of New York City. Early in his childhood, Jay was surrounded by musical influences. His parents' wide-ranging record collection was seminal in the development of Jay's "encyclopedic knowledge of records":

> My mother introduced me to funk. My dad was really into jazz but also, while at college, got into rock, Nazareth, Cream, Jack Bruce, all these different groups, Hendrix, that sort of stuff. So when I was growing up, those records were around the house.

In addition to recordings, Jay's extended family dabbled in music, providing him easy access to a smattering of instruments and ample opportunity to "bang around" with family members.

> My family were all amateur musicians. At my grandma's house in Queen's, we had an organ. We had an old jazz bop drum kit there. We had a flute, a trumpet, a sax. I got a guitar for Christmas. I played trombone in the school band. I played violin. Between music in school, my grandmother's on weekends, and just banging on stuff, I played a little bit of everything.

One instrument "really spoke to" Jay. At age 10, he became enthralled with "messing around with and learning" bass guitar. Inspired by funk music, Jay hoped to form a band; however, "in the late '80s, funk was kind of passé." Jay recalled making a conscious decision to pivot:

> By the time I was 13 or 14, I had gotten really good on the bass. I was in the school jazz band. I played upright bass in the orchestra but I wanted to form my own band to play funk. Thing was, I couldn't find a band outside of school. So I had to do something different.

Without other musicians to play with, Jay "got into hip hop because they were sampling the funk records" he used to practice bass. He recalled:

> I remember, I was like, 'Well that's something I could do myself. I don't have to start a band.' So I kind of pursued hip hop production at a young age. I guess I was 14 or 15 at the time.

Adaptability, in the face of shifting trends in music, has remained a primary engine for Jay's musical development, which has followed a mercurial pattern. The pattern follows like so. Jay surveys what's happening in a given music scene. He figures out where his abilities fit in or have value to others. He then identifies and develops new abilities to meet emerging opportunities, making him "a jack of many trades."

Although Jay identified as a jack of many trades, studio-based production, in one form or another, seemed to be the thread that binds his various musical endeavors. As a teenager, Jay noted that the DJs he admired in the late '80s did more than spin records. They provided the backbone for rappers, the form, structure, and other architectural elements of the rap music of the day. Many DJs transitioned from performative DJing, providing live breaks, beats, and mixes for rappers, to studio-based production that mimicked their live DJing techniques. Jay recalled taking note of those developments:

> Most of the hip hop producers at the time, their port of entry was DJing. They were usually a DJ for a group. They wound up by default becoming the producer because they knew records. When the group they worked with did well, other people would seek the DJ out for production. Guys like DJ Premier or Pete Rock or DJ Mugs or Bomb Squad with Public Enemy, like those were the guys that I was listening to.

Those observations prompted Jay to go "where the producers were." At the age of 15, Jay connected with Power Play Studios, a now legendary hip-hop studio that was located in Queens, New York. He started as an intern but his willingness to learn, "to do what it takes," to be flexible in the face of necessity, ingratiated him with the studio personnel.

> So when I was 15, I decided to go in a different direction. I got an internship at Power Play Studios in Queens. It was a hip hop studio and Large Professor, a renowned hip hop producer, he basically discovered Nas and produced a lot of classic stuff; he was working on some albums there. I would take out the trash, get food from a restaurant, sweep the bathroom floor. I'd work in the reel to reel room but like they wouldn't

let me touch the equipment. Basically, I went in there like, "hey, I just want to learn." At the end of each day, I would go in the session and watch them record. When I saw Large Professor using an SP-1200 sampling drum machine, I knew I wanted one!

That experience prompted Jay to look for access to the SP-1200 and to other sampling devices popular in the late '80s and early '90s. Like many other producers, Jay became "obsessed with getting [his] hands on different machines."

A few years later, at the age of 17, Jay landed another internship with legendary producer Vance Wright. Jay recalled his time working at Wright's studio as "my most important educational experience, maybe even more than college." Jay described the environment, rich with learning opportunities, and a willing mentor:

I got an internship with Vance Wright, Slick Rick's DJ. It was a local studio with Brand Nubian, and all these different people, Digable Planets came in. It was a small studio, like Power Play, so it didn't take long for me to learn the equipment. Vance let me watch the sessions. He let me peer over his shoulder. I would take notes. By the time I started my senior year of high school [autumn of 1994], I was a full-time engineer. I would get paid [chuckles]. I was doing all these sessions. I would go to school, get on a bus, go into the studio, four days during the week, and then weekends, Friday, Saturday night. I would be there 9 or 10 hours. I'd get there at 4:00 PM on a Friday and leave at 4:00 AM. Twelve hour sessions. I really cut my teeth. I learned all my production and engineering chops. I didn't go to school for any of that. By the time I got to college, I already had a lot of engineering chops. I already had production chops.

Jay attended college, studying music and music production. Although he came in with a lot of knowledge, Jay learned a tremendous amount at school, although much of what he learned came from experiences external to the curriculum.

While at college, Jay had one professor that to this day he counts as a mentor. Nonetheless, Jay credits most of his university education to mistakes, social interactions, and the juxtaposition of his life's experiences against and among those of students from vastly different cultural, racial, social, and musical backgrounds. He reflected on his years as an undergraduate:

I learned by making mistakes. I just learned by experience, like trial by fire. It wasn't anything I learned in class, it was because of my classmates. You know, you're a hip hop guy. You're in the hip hop world, in a hip hop studio, and you're a music major at college. The girl sitting next to you plays folk music. The guy next to her plays electronic music. Another person's a jazz guitarist. I soaked up things from other musicians playing other genres. That was how I developed my own production style.

Jay drew on the eclecticism of campus, of his classmates, and of their varied musical expertise. Drawing from each of their "individual sounds," Jay developed his own "identity as a producer." He recalled:

When I got to college I was making beats that sounded like my favorite productions. I didn't have an identity. By the time I graduated, I had an identity. It was like you're coming in with this hip hop background but you're in class with people who do all this different stuff, and you're like, "Wow!"' like "You did something in 5/4." Like 5/4 is not a hip hop time signature [chuckling]. You start experimenting with 5/4 because the kids in a rock band, they did something in 5/4. So, the one thing formal education did for me was put me around people who did different things.

Today, Jay continues to develop his musicianship by adapting to circumstance, pivoting in response to shifting paradigms or because he gets "frustrated" and wants to try something else or get around an obstacle.

As sampling preexisting recordings became an expensive and legally treacherous undertaking, Jay pivoted again and began "really working on drumming." His goal was to learn drumming so that he could reproduce breaks, loops, and beats reminiscent of the vintage funk, R&B, and soul drummers so prevalent in hip-hop production. Such adaptability in the face of shifting trends in music has remained the primary engine in Jay's music learning. Jay surmised:

I have tried to develop as many skills as I can. A lot of that comes from survival, a lot of it came from necessity. You know, coming up, my goal was to be a hip hop producer. Now, I'm sort of a triple threat, drummer, DJ/Producer, and rapper [laughing]. The bad thing is I don't feel like I have enough hours in the day to master any of my crafts. The good thing is if I get frustrated with something, which happens easily, I can work on something else [laughing]. You know, so at this point, like I'm kind of doing everything [laughing].

Jakub Smith

At 19, Jakub Smith, a State Trooper in training, enjoys a bustling side career as a bluegrass musician. From Jakub's description of his experiences, it seems many Appalachian folk musicians live similarly dual lives, working at one thing during the week and traveling the bluegrass and Appalachian folk music circuit on weekends and holidays, "traveling all over the East Coast, from North Carolina to Kentucky to West Virginia to Virginia, even up to Pennsylvania in Gettysburg, going to different bluegrass festivals and meeting people."

All in the Family

Partly out of an insatiable love for music and partly out of necessity, Jakub plays "the banjo, the bass, the guitar, pretty much any string instrument, depending on the needs of my fellow musicians." Those fellow musicians include a wide array of family, friends, and acquaintances ranging from Jakub's grandparents in rural West Virginia to regionally known touring acts with which Jakub has performed, recorded, or jammed at bluegrass and folk music festivals.

Jakub learned from his grandparents. Although he grew up in Westminster, Maryland, Jakub spent a good deal of time visiting his paternal grandparents in rural West Virginia. His grandparents had quite a bluegrass pedigree from which Jakub could draw inspiration and practical *Hee Haw* knowledge. He explained:

> My grandparents, John and Sue Smith, have traveled all over playing bluegrass music with people like Earl Scruggs. I'm pretty sure they played on the television show. My grandparents played on the same show that Earl Scruggs played on. They played with Paul Williams and The Victory Trio. They're bluegrass and they're gospel musicians, so they've really transferred that to me. They played for greater than 40 years. They actually met on, I think it was on WBAO or some crazy old time radio station in the hills of West Virginia, like back in the '40s. So they've been at it for a while [laughing].

Although a relative novice compared to his grandparents, Jakub has spent more than half of his young life in bluegrass music. From an early age, Jakub "sat at [his] grandfather's knee, maybe 6 or so, and just listen[ed] to him play banjo." Jakub recalled moments when his grandfather let him pluck around on the banjo and then on a mandolin, and a guitar, "just to get the feel of the strings." By "10 or 11," Jakub began playing stringed instruments, especially the string bass, more seriously.

Prior to taking up bluegrass, Jakub studied some classical piano and participated in youth music programs, most notably "kinder music," a program for small children and their parents that Jakub credits with helping encourage his ability to 'play by ear'. Like a lot of teens, Jakub also plays music popular among his peer group, including rock, alternative rock, and some classic rock, "but really it's the bluegrass that's been the constant." And bluegrass, for Jakub, seems bound up with his grandparents.

Mentors

The importance of Jakub's grandparents in his musical development cannot be overstated. Throughout our discussion, Jakub referred to his grandfather's tutelage, his grandmother's encouragement, and his grandparents' network of friends, all of whom played bluegrass, country, and other Appalachian folk musics such as "old timey string stuff." Jakub explained:

> I was like I said before I was around my grandparents who are musicians and they play a lot of music. All their friends play too so it provided me with a bunch of contacts, people who already knew me when I would go to jam sessions or to festivals. Sometimes I would meet people at festivals and they would be like, "oh you're John's and Sue's grandson," and I'd just be in.

When pressed about how his grandparents mentored him, Jakub was a bit at a loss, commenting,

> that's a really good question. Well, I mean there wasn't really a set of skills that I needed to learn as much as my grandparents showed me how to do something and then let me do it with other, more experienced musicians.

Jakub's experience learning by doing echoed similar statements from other MLPP participants. Yet, when pressed further, Jakub began describing some very specific skills, reflecting, for example, that:

> There were definitely some, there were finger positions, and, well for the bass, there were finger positions, and like how to keep perfect time on the bass. So it's very simple, so I guess . . . he was preparing me to play other instruments without me even knowing it.

Those specific skills, coupled with the immersion experiences afforded by jamming with his grandparents and their network of musician friends, helped Jakub make professional contacts that transformed him from part-time enthusiast to sought-after professional.

Later in the conversation, Jakub summed up the cumulative impact of his grandparent's mentoring and the lasting influence of the experiences their network of friends provided:

> Let's say I go up to Gettysburg and I'll go to a festival, it's easy to follow along with different people. I know everything from memory. I don't need a book or anything like that. I can just sit down and start playing, which to me, is extremely natural but to other people, it's just, "Well, how can you do this?" It just, it allows me to, I guess, be more confident. Like with the guys, when I practice with them, if they say a song, I automatically know it and can play it. Like it might need a little bit of tweaking but hey, it's still there. It's still available to me. I can do it. I know the sound. All these different songs, and different chord progressions, I know 'em automatically, just from playing. I don't need a recording. I don't need a book. It's just automatic, and even if it's something new, I can pick it up within five minutes and it'll be stage quality.

Music Education

Jakub's ascent into professional musicianship started with "certain aspects" of his music education. Jakub recalled enjoying kinder music, piano lessons, and school music "to an extent," but after elementary general music, Jakub found little of interest in the school music programs offered at his high school. He explained:

> In high school, I took time off from music education, at least as far as school or lessons. I still did jam sessions but I didn't take any music classes because, well because there's no, there's not really a spot for a banjo player in a band or a choir or anything.

Fortunately for Jakub, his school music teachers were sympathetic and responsive to his situations. Sensing his burgeoning skill, the teachers and administrators at Jakub's high school approved an independent study. Jakub explained:

> When my senior year came along, I was approved for an independent study with the choir director. I was able to play with the girls' choir when they did country songs. I would help assist in teaching theory because I knew basic theory and also, I was able to play different songs, on the banjo *and* on the piano, for them when they performed their

concerts. Actually for the banjo, the director never gave me any sheet music. She just gave me the song and was like, "here, play it!" And [chuckling], I was like, "okay! I can do that."

Jakub, who at the time of this writing had just started post-secondary studies at a community college, took some music appreciation courses. He hoped to "take some theory too, but music will only be a part of my studies, between studying and playing on weekends, there's only so much time."

Through his grandparents Jakub met members of the Appalachian folk group Black Diamond, including brothers Eddie and Tom Marrs, well known on the Appalachian folk music festival scene. Eddie and Tom, as well as the members of their band, became de facto mentors to Jakub. Jakub described their influence:

Those guys, I really looked up to them and they were like, really like my grandparents. Every time I would go down to my grandparents, we would have jam sessions. And every year, you know, they would also be there. Eddie the banjo player would show me different rolls, different licks that I could catch and over the years, it just started building until I got this whole collection in my memory of all these different rolls.

Those experiences afforded Jakub the confidence to go in "as a teenager and sit in with much older, more experienced players." The confidence, the skillset, and Jakub's growing knowledge of Appalachian folk music repertoire led to additional opportunities.

Today, Jakub plays with the band Aspen Run, comprised of musicians well known on the bluegrass circuit, ones Jakub "looks up to." He is well known in the bluegrass circuit as a go-to bass player with rock solid time. As he approaches 20, he thinks he'd like to encourage and even mentor "the next generation" the way his grandparents and their friends nurtured him. Jakub offered the following advice for other "youngsters," like himself looking to break into bluegrass and Appalachian folk music:

You cannot really go to school or to a college and learn how to do this. You definitely have to talk to people, elders who have had the music, who know the music, who know what they're doing, who know every little part, who have watched other musicians. They can pass that down to you. You have to learn that way. Any other way doesn't really, isn't really bluegrass. There's a type of soul reaction. You have to love the music to be able to play. Listen to a lot of recordings but also go meet people. Listen and ask to sit in, even if you only play a small part at first.

It has to be taught aurally. Like, inadvertently, like just one generation to the next. Just like my grandfather's father played the banjo, and he taught my grandfather how to play guitar. My grandfather then taught himself how to play the banjo too. You have to find somewhere in the hills of Appalachia or in the hills of West Virginia, or somewhere in the south, be someone who really enjoys the music, enjoys being around the music.

Robert Ray Boyette

Robert Ray Boyette, a 19-year-old from Greensboro, North Carolina, started emulating rhythms using his mouth and voice "somewhere around six years old." What started as "original, unorthodox" vocalizing along with Robert's favorite music evolved into a highly idiosyncratic practice, "vocal percussion emulation of prog and metal drummers." Today, Robert enjoys an online reputation as a master beatboxer.

Idiosyncratic Virtuoso

Beatboxers are musicians who use their voices, mouths, breath, and sometimes bodies to recreate percussive musical passages (Garfield, 2002). Although beatboxing has been a core element of hip-hop from its earliest history, the practice has expanded, appearing in and influencing other forms of popular music singing. Just the same, beatboxing has been influenced by many other musical practices, resulting in new hybridized approaches celebrated at international beatbox competitions, posted online, and employed by a cappella singing groups.

Robert has pioneered his own unique hybrid approach, beatboxing the sounds and technical virtuosity of progressive rock drumming. Despite, or perhaps owing to, developing such a specific focus, Robert has become something of a celebrity, publishing performance videos online, some garnering as many as half a million views. In each of his video performances, roboyette, as he's known online, produces, records, and performs elaborate beatboxed versions of dizzyingly complex prog rock (progressive rock) drum tracks.

His virtuosity is remarkable. For example, roboyette's most popular video to date features a beatbox interpretation of "The Dance of Eternity," a song by the US progressive rock band Dream Theatre. The original recording, which features renowned drummer Mike Portnoy, includes some 108 time signature changes. roboyette reproduced Portnoy's drumming beat for beat, sound for sound, and marked each of the time changes by holding flashcards up to the camera. The video became somewhat of a sensation, widely distributed among online drumming and beatboxing communities.

Learning on His Own

Mike Portnoy took note of roboyette's vocal percussion interpretation of the song, sharing the video with millions of online fans and furthering Rob's already burgeoning popularity. Remarkably, despite "a huge passion for music," Robert had "never received any formal music lessons . . . for singing, or [his] special interest in vocal percussion." Robert explained the genesis of his idiosyncratic approach to vocal percussion:

> From the time I was like six years old, I just liked to make music with my mouth, singing, beatboxing, and tapping rhythms with my hands, music with my body, really. It was all oral, and I guess aural too, I would hear a song, like I was really into dance music, I guess music that I thought was kind of cool or hip to dance to, and I would just sort of do the rhythms with my mouth.

Robert continued to hone this "somewhat odd ability" in private, as a way to entertain himself. Sometimes he'd beatbox to music while studying, or in response to the theme music from his favorite television programs, to make his family or friends laugh, or to add "percussive accents to songs [he] would sing along with." He explained his process:

> I guess, really, I just kept practicing. I just kept doing it. I heard myself. I just kept trying to work on what I thought sounded cool and to expand the way I sounded into something that was closer to what I was hearing on recordings or closer to what I wanted to hear. It was sort of like a combination of both. My basses got hard and my snares got sharper and the rhythms got simpler, simpler for me to do.

Along the way, Rob added to his palette of sounds, playing with "different textures, new rhythms, just anything, you know, experimenting, and trying to emulate different sounds." He recalled emulating the sounds of "quads or quints," the array of toms favored by US drum corps. Reproducing those sounds added a melodic element to Rob's craft. At this point in his young life, roughly age 14, Rob began to specialize, focusing on the music he loved most. He explained:

> I really liked progressive music, complex music, rhythmically complex, anything with very intense complex drum lines and I started to come across a lot of music like that. I'm really interested in doing emulations of the drums with my voice, so beatbox covers of progressive rock and progressive metal drummers seemed like a challenge.

Rob had little idea of the attention his experimentation with beatboxing would eventually garner. To this point, most of Rob's vocal percussion was ephemeral, done in the moment, singing out loud to himself or with family and friends.

As his preferred repertoire grew in complexity, Robert would "sometimes use a digital voice record to record and listen to parts or sounds." The recorder helped Robert recall increasingly complex rhythms and newly developed techniques for producing certain vocal percussion sounds. Eventually, he started to experiment with recording software and with video. His intent was "never to share what I was doing as much as to great something I could listen back to but then I realized what I had was maybe a little unique." At that point, roughly around age 16, Robert decided to post his first video. The video would be the one that would eventually garner a million and a half views, the attention of Mike Portnoy, Dream Theatre, and prog rock fans the world over. The video also caused a stir in the beatbox community, where it was shared in beatboxing forums, online communities, and websites.

Ironically, Robert never thought of what he was doing as "beatboxing." Although he sometimes shared his ability with family and close friends, he was unaware of beatboxing, its history, or the sizeable online communities that celebrate the practice. Rob explained:

> I had never heard of beatboxing before, not until years after I had started doing it. I didn't even know what to call it. I just sort of emulated the drums, the rhythm of a track, with my mouth, whatever it was. It was an original, or at least unorthodox, way of doing it.

Robert repeatedly described developing his beatboxing "mostly by myself," in private, "without any real connection to the beatboxing community." In fact, Robert recalled learning about internet beatboxing communities "only after Dance of Eternity became a thing." He explained:

> There was nobody else really that gave me guidance or advice and I didn't do it in any sort of public setting and I didn't really listen to that much music that would have facilitated a lot of exploration of that, of beatboxing.

Although he learned largely by himself, Robert did "share ideas" with two other people, his older brother and his closest friend, both of whom would beatbox with Robert "from time to time."

Robert's older brother was less serious about vocal percussion. He would do some of it here or there but always in "response" to Robert's "new sound or technique." Robert explained:

> My brother would hear my beatboxing and he would, he tried it for a little while, and he was okay, but he never got to the level I was at,

but he would sort of give pointers as to like how I could sound cooler or whatever [laughs]. One of the things I remember, he liked my bass drum sound but wanted it to sound fuller or darker, louder, to have more umph behind the bass or whatever, and so that kind of inspired a different kind of way that I'd do that.

Robert's friend worked with him "kind of like a percussionist works with a drum set player, providing percussive accents to songs" or to Robert's beatboxing. Consequently, some of Robert's friends' sounds, which "were more color or accent type sounds" made their way into or at least influenced Robert's palette of percussion sounds.

Transition to School

At the time of this writing, Robert had enrolled in the Ohio State University with the intention of studying music. Although he did not have musical training as a child, he began to become more serious about music making in his adolescence, a shift he attributes, at least partly, to his interest in vocal percussion. As a teenager, Robert began participating in musical theater; singing, acting, and interacting with other teens provided him with "confidence to do things like share the beatboxing videos." At the Ohio State University, Robert studies singing and guitar, and he participates in the University's acclaimed a cappella group, Buck That!, where he's found a new "home for vocal percussion." Aside from the initial video posts that garnered him so much attention, Robert has done fewer "vocal percussion cover videos" than he had anticipated as he concentrates on his continuing music studies.

Mike Amari

Mike Amari described his life's work as "all pretty much music related. Everything kind of interacts with the other things." Everything includes singing, songwriting, playing guitar, recording music, performing music, playing drums, and working as the talent buyer for BSP Kingston, a small music venue in New York's Hudson Valley, some 90 miles north of New York City.

Keeping His Day Job

Mike speaks about BSP Kingston, or his "occupation," with enthusiasm. Where some musicians might see a day job as a hindrance to their musical aspirations, Mike sees BSP as an extension. The connections between his occupation and his musical aspirations are many. Mike referred to them repeatedly throughout our interview. His work at the venue is multi-faceted, putting him in touch with musicians, management companies, and other contacts that have helped him further his own musical endeavors. Mike explained:

> As far as my occupation goes, I'm the talent buyer at a small music venue. It holds about 200 people, in Kingston, NY. So what I do there is I handle all the booking requests. I also reach out to a lot of people. I set up shows. I handle all of the sort of pre-production that goes into the show. I'll handle online promotion and physical promotion, radio promotion, various types of marketing, all of our social media, and I also do a lot on the day of a show, you know, in terms of hospitality for the bands and setting up the venue and even helping bands load in and set sometimes. I see huge intersections between the music community I'm in and this job as a talent buyer. Musicians I book—just by them seeing that I'm responsible, that I'm accountable—become interested in continuing to work together. That might be playing a show together, helping me get a show in whatever area they're from. For me, that community of musicians is all one in the same. I'll have interactions with the same person, some of it will be about a show we're playing together. Some of it will be about the record label they run. Some of it will be about a show I booked with an artist on their label. It's all one big conversation, as I see it.

As he described his work, Mike switched back and forth between his work as a talent buyer and his work as a musician, bandleader, and audio producer. After describing his work at the venue, Mike continued:

> So, that's my job description but I'm also a working musician. I play in three different bands. One of the bands I play in is, I would say, more

serious than the others; we tour around the States and we're supposed to do this tour in Europe in a couple of months and we do sort of all the full-fledged band stuff in that project. I do all that.

He then pivoted back to the talent buying work, citing some of the freelance booking assignments he's taken on in recent years:

> I get hired as a talent buyer for a couple of local music festivals in the Hudson Valley region. I'll help them secure bands for their festivals and work out contracts and things like this. It's all pretty much music related, which is really nice. It all kinds of interacts with the other things. Each different thing that I work on kind of helps the other things that I work on.

Each thing Mike does has impacted the others from his earliest memories, although he didn't always see things that way. The spate of endeavors that comprise Mike's musical life started to coalesce in adolescence.

Industrious Creativity

Mike's an industrious character by nature, starting to write songs, record, and perform as an adolescent in "South Jersey, not too far from Philadelphia." Supportive family figured prominently into Mike's explanations of how he got started in music. Mike recalled:

> My parents started me with piano lessons when I was like 8 or 9. I didn't really like it [chuckles] but I definitely recognized later on, as I was learning guitar, and as I took music theory in high school and college, that piano theory, those basic skills really came in handy.

After tolerating a few years of piano lessons, Mike became interested in the guitar, his "primary instrument." He learned largely on his own, taking some lessons here or there, but relied more on years of self-guided experimentation. Mike's experiences with guitar seem to have informed his creative ethos: "learn the basics of whatever it is you want to do. There's some technical things you should know but then do your own thing through a lot experimentation. After all some of the best music is the simplest."

Mike learned to record and use studio gear, and he further developed his musicianship in a recording studio near his childhood home. An uncle affiliated with the studio, housed on the campus of a Philadelphia university, provided Mike access to what would become a creative safe haven. Mike described his experiences there:

> I had an uncle who worked at a local university, in the engineering department. One of the things they were really interested in was audio engineering and so they offered a few courses related to that and they built a small studio. They had a small Pro Tools rig and a couple of microphones. He gave me a basic understanding of Pro Tools and then toward the end of my time in high school, when I got my license to drive and a car, my uncle gave me a key to the studio, so I learned very hands-on with Pro Tools, and various micing techniques, and recording all sorts of stuff from digital synthesizers to analog instruments and even, at that point, doing a little of drumming myself, and all the micing that goes along with that. So, I learned very hands on that way.

Mike's parents, noting his growing engagement with recording, suggested he enroll in a recording workshop at a Philadelphia university, one that offered courses in music business, as well as recording. Mike recalled that experience as particularly influential:

> My parents were sort of researching the music industry thing, as a career option, which I didn't even know about. They made me aware of a week-long summer program at Drexel University that I did before my senior year in high school, right around the same time I was applying to colleges. That course gave me a more universal understanding of Pro Tools as an application. It introduced me to things like looping and sampling, things I hadn't used already.

The support of his parents played a role in Mike's university education. His parents suggested that he major in music industry. On his own, he was considering "a business degree or something [he] didn't really care about." His parents argued that he should pick a major that "merged [Mike's] interest in music with a sort of business approach."

Mike's studies at SUNY Oneonta provided additional background and would play an important role in his current professional life. At the college, some 150 miles north and west of New York City, far from Mike's south Jersey upbringing, he studied the music industry, including courses in marketing, merchandising, and communications.

Mike's industrious creativity was evident in a project that merged his recording, performing, and music industry studies. For years, Mike has recorded under the name Lovesick. While at SUNY Oneonta, Mike released a Lovesick album for which he created a multi-faceted marketing campaign that included merchandising in local shops, touring, media promotion, and other creative branding efforts. Oneonta provided Mike with many opportunities to perform. He would use his burgeoning music business savvy to put together bills with multiple bands, to promote those events, and to network. Mike recalled:

> So that was really how I got started, putting together shows in college with my own bands, getting into the idea of "Oh, we need to make a poster for this show" and just making it and putting it around in the right shops or whatever. It just came to me. I put a lot of effort into the shows I booked. It came naturally.

The team that operates BSP Kingston also has roots at SUNY Oneonta. Mike recalled their early interactions, noting that in college, they were somewhat unaware of each other:

> It's funny because me and the other guys at BSP, we worked together without realizing it in college. We'd play shows together in our respective bands. We would promote events together. In fact, they put on a music festival for a couple of years that ended up being as big as 1,000 or 1,200 people. It started very small and I had helped them a little with that.

Shortly after graduation, Mike found himself working with the same crew, people who had been acquaintances at college now became Mike's closest working colleagues.

The management of BSP Kingston offered Mike an opportunity to try booking, presenting, and promoting shows at the venue on a sort of trial basis. That trial afforded Mike the opportunity to "learn on the fly." He recalled the process unfolding from nothing:

> I really started from scratch. My friends, who were also from Oneonta, took over a venue. They did some renovating, put in a great sound system. They were just putting in a lot of effort. I saw all the effort but sort of a lack of knowledge and wherewithal, in terms of the booking at least, so I started doing a weekly residency there, every Tuesday night, and it was doing very well so we added Thursday nights, and soon after that, I just took over all of the booking.

As Mike developed the booking calendar, so too developed his network of connections. His own music career, as a songwriter, guitarist, and eventually drummer, blossomed. He recalled how things grew from that point with a bit of wonder, some surprise, and enthusiasm for his future:

> It snowballed pretty quickly. Especially with the musicians I was book-ing. Musicians telling other musicians "this is a great place to play. Work with this guy." And that word of mouth pretty quickly led to booking like national or international acts like Sean Lennon and Kurt Vile. It all happened pretty quickly. You know the first six months were pretty much only local musicians. The last year though, pretty quickly, it's taken off.

Beyond BSP, Mike plays as one half of the duo Shana Falana, named for its founder, also profiled in the MLPP. As in all areas of his musical life, Mike wears many hats with Shana Falana, playing drums, doing production, overseeing aspects of the band's tech heavy performances, and shouldering a fair share of the band's booking, touring logistics, and promotion. Mike described the technical aspects of Shana Falana's performances:

> We remix studio tracks from Shana's recordings, mixing them a little differently, you know, a little more appropriate for a live setting. Some backing tracks we've recorded ourselves, at home, in various ways. We run all that stuff through a Pro Tools rig when we play live. We have an in ear click that keeps us locked up to everything. So, when we per-form, we bring a whole computer set up and extra amplifiers that you probably wouldn't see with a two person band. We set up a whole drum kit. Shana also does live looping with her vocals and guitar. It ends up sounding pretty big. It's a kind of thick wall of sound thing that we do, with just two people.

Shana Falana tours the US, has toured Europe, and continues to release music as of this writing. Mike summarized, "between the stuff with Shana, BSP, and my own projects, it's pretty much a musical life. I'm really fortu-nate to be able to say that."

Jacquelyn Hynes

Jacquelyn is a musician and actor, and primarily a flutist. She is a performer, writer, teacher and activist. I have known her for several years, since we performed on tour together with the London-based psycho-ceilidh (folk-punk) band, Neck. Jacquelyn is in her 40s, and is committed to performing; as she states: "performing is still the priority, I haven't grown out of that yet . . . I do quite a lot of gigging." She emphasizes the centrality of performing to her life, saying that "you feel like you're being unfaithful" (if you don't prioritize performing): "that's really what it's about for me, and everything else is about that. And the times when I have prioritized teaching, it's always been a mistake; I've always missed an opportunity, or seemed to miss an opportunity." Jacquelyn's career and her outlook are characterized by restlessness and a commitment to artistic growth. As she says, "all I ever wanted to do was play the flute, play the piano, and act, and that's largely been what I've done, really."

Career

> I don't think I ever had a plan . . . I always thought you'd find out so much as you went along, really, and you do—you certainly find out what you don't want to do, and you get deep into something you do want to do, I guess.

Here Jacquelyn captures the essence of her dedication to her art, and her approach to that dedication—allowing her muse to lead her, rather than making meticulous arrangements for her future.

Jacquelyn has for many years played music extensively as part of the Irish 'trad' folk scene in London—she jokes: "my father grew up in an Irish pub, and it's interesting that I end up back there quite a lot of the time." A key development in Jacquelyn's career is how she has gradually learned "to say 'yes' to more things," including playing in Neck—having "said no a few times" to the repeated requests of the band's leader, she then agreed to perform with the band—"that's something you learn".

Jacquelyn's career has often involved the close interaction of music performance and acting. She once joined a touring theatre company, looking to pursue a career in acting. She found, however, that theatre mostly involved music, and she points to how working as an actor was beneficial for developing musical skills such as timing and "feeling the moment." A theatrical perspective helps her to see the flute as a character or protagonist when she is writing and performing with the instrument. As well as seeing similarities between arts, Jacquelyn perceives similarities, rather than distinctions, between various musics as well, suggesting that, for instance, "a cadenza is a jazz solo, you know."

Jacquelyn writes and performs music with Avalonia, an eclectic ensemble comprised of musicians from various oral traditions including Indian, Irish, and Arabian musics, among which improvisation is the shared practice. She expresses amazement at the Indian singer's ability to reproduce every tonal inflection of (other) traditions, for instance performing Irish music in the Irish language and with the feel and idiosyncrasies of that style. She describes herself as being like "an amoeba" that absorbs music from all these other influences, and then they turn up in something that she writes. She finds that she is getting deeper into music, and that this means focusing on one's own practice. She can hear others' influences in her playing as well: "you are a product of all your influences, unconsciously as well as consciously."

Jacquelyn says that "what you want changes," and thus she has always sought new challenges and different experiences: "I'm always looking for new things, trying new things—I've got a very low boredom threshold, really; although the deeper you dive into something, the less bored you get." Thus for her, living and learning in music are closely intertwined. Emphasizing this point, Jacquelyn urges,

> I think, really, to pursue a career as a performer, what you have to have is this overwhelming sense that you really have, as far as you know, one time on the merry-go-round, and you want to find out as much as you can.

Learning

Jacquelyn describes a life dedicated to learning, developing, and improving, in self-directed ways, and with the guidance of others. As she says, "you kind of educate yourself, don't you, but with the help of amazing people along the way." She recalls that when she was about 8 years old, her parents bought a piano for Jacquelyn and her sister. Her mother was "naturally musical," and played piano by ear—a form of music learning that was to become central to Jacquelyn's journey.

Jacquelyn has taken music lessons from numerous people throughout her life (although she has "never paid for music lessons"), and has stayed in touch with many of these, seeing her growth in music as a very interpersonal journey She received free tuition on piano and flute at her school, giving her a "good classical grounding, although I wouldn't regard myself as a classical musician." "My piano teacher when I was eight was fantastically musical . . . full of music and love, I thought she was extraordinary and all my piano teachers since then". Another strong influence was a flute teacher, Jenny, because of "the quality of the sound, and the passion of the teacher" who is "just so in love with the flute." Jacquelyn feels incredibly grateful that "all the music teachers I had were really funny, really alive, just really great people" who continue to motivate and inspire her to pursue a life in music.

She recalls: "I resented being educated a lot of the time; I thought a lot of it was a waste of time." Music was the exception to this, because of having such inspiring teachers. Her high school English teacher played electric guitar and jammed with students in corridors during lunch hours, and it was here that Jacquelyn learned to improvise, and where she learned (that it was okay) to combine music and activism through writing and performing for peers on an anti-war theme (this was during the Falklands conflict).

Jacquelyn studied performing arts as an undergraduate at Middlesex Polytechnic, with an interest primarily in drama, since she felt she "could already play music," having been "putting together different combos and playing with them since age of 12." While at college, she performed in public on a weekly basis with a ceilidh band, as well as with the college's contemporary music ensemble at concert venues. She points to these experiences teaching her a lot about rhythm. Jacquelyn was then funded through a scholarship to complete an MA in Irish Music, on which all teaching and learning was done orally/aurally. Immersing herself in this tradition was a transformative experience.

Skills and Attributes

Whilst having a highly developed skill set as a professional musician and actor, Jacquelyn finds it tricky to articulate the skills that she possesses, preferring to focus instead on things she does. She describes performing with a strong sense of being present, saying:

> You definitely get in to a special zone when you're performing, I think, which is akin to a religious experience or a sports sense of flow . . . it's an altered state, and I don't think anyone can touch it, and once you've had it you crave it and crave it and crave it and you just want to be there all the time really. It's very difficult to come off it.

Jacquelyn suggests that the only necessary skill she possesses for her career is:

> A lack of imagination, in some ways . . . bloody-mindedness, having no knowledge that money was important or even relevant . . . I remember realizing at 17 you could either have things or do things. That was a clear choice, and I decided to do things . . . I don't have the skills that you need—dealing with money, administration.

This clarity of purpose has been present in her life for many years:

> I was a rebel at school, I failed all my O levels. Just not being interested in anything else, I think that helped—just only being interested in music and theatre. Sometimes it's more theatre than music; it's much more music than theatre at the moment . . . there's nothing else that's continuous in my life—apart from my family, I suppose. It's like my religion, my mission, my everything—I wouldn't get up if I didn't have it to do.

This devotion to her art and to learning has been sufficient.

Passing It On

There is a sense of generosity and humility to the way that Jacquelyn approaches the passing on of the musical baton. She says, "I try to be one tenth as good as the teachers who taught me." Jacquelyn's advice for the next generation draws on her own experience, and is grounded perhaps equally in personal insecurities as in confidence. She produced several pithy sound bites of counsel in our interview:

> It [life as a musician] is a bit of a pilgrimage for the soul, because you just have to really pursue your own path, and you've got to be able to live with yourself;
>
> There's always a tension between tradition and innovation;
>
> The only thing that will make a difference is practicing, and your relationship with the instrument;
>
> You learn a lot about performing from doing it;
>
> You learn everything on the job;
>
> If you try to reproduce a brilliant improvised moment, you can't. What you need to do is to reproduce the conditions that allowed that to happen so you can allow it to happen spontaneously;
>
> It's tough, being a performer;
>
> You definitely get back what you give out in music.

Following on from this last point, Jacquelyn likes to improvise and play with people with all levels of musical experience, feeling that we can each learn from anyone. She warms to an 'egalitarian' way of playing and learning in the aural Irish folk music tradition, which welcomes, nurtures, and celebrates engagement from musicians at all levels, from novices to the highly experienced.

Jacquelyn teaches flute at two institutions—one where she works with young people, and another where she works with adults returning to education. In the latter context she teaches beginner flute classes through (mostly Irish) folk music, and teaches by ear to remain authentic to the tradition, and because when learning by ear "they actually have to learn the music." Jacquelyn feels strongly that this 'aurality' is an important skill for musicians, including in classical music where listening skills are traditionally taught as additional or supplementary to the core performance skill set.

Jacquelyn worries that music education is "becoming a middle-class playground, but you shouldn't hold anyone's background against them, and they still ought to be respected as an artist if they are an artist." Beyond education, she is "trying to make a little difference, in a little way. I always assumed I'd be world-famous, and then go and work for UNICEF or something." She works not for UNICEF but in a high-profile role with the UK Musicians' Union, on the London Regional Committee, and as Chair of the Equalities Committee. Her work has highlighted a need to mentor and support older musicians, identifying "fantastically talented people heading the wrong way." She also feels that arts advocacy needs to shift its focus from a largely utilitarian discourse, feeling strongly that:

> The arts have a value above and beyond that [making money], really, which is immeasurable . . . and it goes beyond each individual art as well . . . Music is music, at the end of the day—why do we have to keep defining it in other terms, and justifying it by other value systems?

Riduan Zalani

Riduan Zalani is a 32-year-old Singaporean Malay musician, specializing in performing and teaching Malay percussion music, which he has played since the age of seven. He is the artistic director of Nadi Singapura, a professional ensemble focused on championing traditional Malay drumming in a contemporary context. Singapore is a multicultural, multiethnic city state, but knowledge and education of traditional Malay music are scarce, in part because citizens of Malay origin are an ethnic minority in the country. Riduan is dedicated to providing teaching and learning in his art and music so that it can thrive for another generation and beyond. For him, this is more than about playing music; he is concerned with keeping Malay cultural identity intact.

Singapore was, at the time of the interview, 50 years old as an independent nation, and Riduan aims to understand the nation's history, such as, for example, when the Portuguese, British, Gujarats, and Arabs arrived, and the impact these visitors had on local community, language, traditions, and culture. From Riduan's perspective, there is little in the arts in Singapore on a policy or government level, despite rhetoric to the contrary; he feels that "culture has been dissipated among the lifestyle of the day," which is primarily focused on the success of the nation's economy through banking and financial services. Further, while the country's leaders are concerned with promoting and preserving some art, they have placed a low priority on Malay culture. Riduan has made it his mission to address this deficit. There are large professional arts organizations for Chinese and Indian musics in Singapore that keep those traditions alive and thriving, with full-time professional musicians offering a range of classes. No comparable professional organization existed for Malay percussion music prior to Riduan's work.

Riduan has travelled to 35 countries making music of various traditions, drawing on drumming of Afro-Brazilian, Latin American, African, Middle Eastern, and oriental traditions. After working with musicians from around the world, he "felt a calling to return to my roots" and co-founded Nadi Singapura with Yaziz Hassan, with whom he had worked as an international performing musician. Yaziz was one of the first people to improvise with and develop Malay drums, introducing a more reliable, mechanical Western-based tuning system for traditional Malay drums, in order to help cope with playing them in climates with dramatically different temperatures and humidity.

Career

Riduan began taking music seriously at age 15 or 16, when he decided to make it a career. Viewing himself as "not smart," he passed his high school exams but failed to complete his studies at polytechnic or at music school, but quickly developed a career as an international performer playing drum kit and percussion. He now performs, composes, arranges, teaches, and studies "everything to do with drums and percussion, leaning closer towards Malay tradition." Riduan formed the Orkestar Trio in 2009 with Mr Ismahairie Putra Ishak and Mr Alhafiz Jamat, comprised of performers playing, respectively, lute and violin, accordion and flute, and percussion and drums. This group has travelled extensively (including Turkey, Malaysia, Indonesia, Hawaii, and Brazil), performing Malay music. This trio, and the larger Nadi Singapura that grew from it, support his trio's vision to create a generation of musicians fluent in Malay music and culture who can "act like a bridge" for the next generation of Malay musicians in Singapore. Riduan manages the only facility in the country that is dedicated to Malay music. Their instruments are made in Malaysia and Indonesia, and developed in Singapore. He also gives a high number of motivational talks and master classes in English—the language with which he struggled in high school—and puts this success down to his interactions around the world as a musician and student of music and culture.

Nadi Singapura has drawn attention to Malay music through presenting large, dramatic performances featuring traditional Malay martial arts and dance. Riduan recalls, "I never thought I would direct segments of national shows, like the national day parade and Chingay. I did my first one when I was 23 years old. When I did the second one, there was about 350 drummers." These initiatives led to the award of the first ever Singapore government grants to continue this work. Nadi Singapura started as part of a community center, and now occupies its own rooms in an arts center in the city.

Learning

Riduan is driven and largely self-taught meaning that "I know what I want to learn and how it can help me, to generating my own sound." Although he aspired to attend California Institute of the Arts, he could not afford the tuition fees, so he sought out lessons and master classes with many musicians. Ultimately, he felt this approach to be preferable because as a student one is able to ask more personally relevant questions of a teacher who knows the students are attending of their own accord. He has tended to spend up to two years focusing on specific instruments or traditions until "eventually it becomes part of you." He was pushed to develop his percussion technique by teachers at LaSalle College of the Arts in Singapore, alongside teachers in classical percussion. LaSalle classes on electroacoustic music led him to incorporate effects and "analogue stuff" into his sound. This college study and his contacts helped him see beyond performance into the ingredients that come together to make a good show, weaving in useful tips from dance, fine arts, and theatre for stage craft and more. He now curates shows and organizes and directs performances. "These contacts and this knowledge . . . give you an edge apart from the others, because you are drummer that directs the show." He did not complete his undergraduate music studies at LaSalle because he felt the curriculum comprised that which others wanted him to learn rather than what he wished to learn. He asserts that "not all education systems are meant for you."

Riduan notes the wide availability of university 'world music' classes globally in, for instance, Indonesian gamelan and African drumming. Arguing that there is nothing intrinsically better about these musics that should warrant the global attention, he aims to promote Malay music, which is far less widely recognized. He wants to "help enhance my culture in Singapore. We were oppressed. I feel that it's time." He now hopes to study for a degree in Malay Arts in order "to learn about everything Malay" from a university in Malaysia. "It's not just about being a musician; everything is one; performance is an art, and with enough aesthetic and artistic value, it becomes really something you cannot push away."

Skills and Attributes

Principal attributes of this successful entrepreneurial musician include a willingness to learn and desire to absorb input from multiple sources. He describes his "pursuit of making connections to the world." He has known many "different teachers for different genres, but I'm the one who decides" what to learn and from whom: "My main teacher is my surroundings and my desire" to learn from anyone whose art interests him. He is currently learning Indian Karnatic studies at Singapore Indian Fine arts institution. He cites his wide network of contacts as a key attribute to his success; people from across disciplines, including theatre, dance, orchestral music, jazz, and experimental music, "are all very supportive of this movement" in Singapore. Other necessary skills for Riduan's work are "patience and belief, a lot of hope." He says, "You need a gangster spirit, like a warrior, never lose out to anything; you have to be open to mistakes, and you must be willing to learn . . . you must be willing to accept your mistakes."

Passing It On

Malay drumming is traditionally taught orally, in a master–apprentice relationship. As such, there is no theory, and no written record of the tradition. Riduan's mission in life is the perpetuation of the Malay music tradition (drumming) in Singapore. He views this as essential, asking with a sense of urgency, "what about the intangible heritage that is not written?" He states that "you need to make sure a particular practice is rightfully understood . . . and that it will breed itself, and you must ensure that it breeds." If people don't do this, we have to go back to ground zero again. "It's important that the community comes together" towards a "unified understanding" of the art. "It's tough" to carry the burden of his cultural identity for a nation. As such, Riduan is part of organizations including the Arts Council, the Youth Council, and the Malay Music Council; on some of these councils he is the only Malay. He feels a weight of responsibility to pass on his culture, so that the next generation is not "left hanging."

> You need to present the craft so it is relatable, it is viewed as a first-class and not as a second-class art practice. It can be for entertainment, but it also needs to have attributes or characters that define you as a community.

Riduan sees his role as in part giving hope to younger musicians, to know that there is someone doing music full-time in Singapore. He says, "if I can do it, you can do it. You can do anything you want, as long as you plan yourself and if you're willing to keep improving and stuff." He gives drumming lessons, but also "people just want to come and hang out." He notes that "a big lot of people have passed through my life," of varying ages. He is called 'Uan-abang'. 'Abang' is big brother; (Rid)Uan is his name. Ordinarily in the Malay tradition, 'abang' comes first, but he is regarded as a special person; "a lot of people define me as an older brother or a teacher or mentor."

He worked with the Singapore Teachers Academy of the Arts (STAR) to create relevant and accessible multimedia curricula on Malay music. Music teachers in Singapore are now required to learn this Malay music as well as Chinese and Indian musics. Riduan feels that learning from history is open to everyone and is ultimately an obligation for students of music, advising,

> Going forward is important, but it's nice to check your back and know a bit more history so you can get further forward . . . whilst you have to be good with the technology that is today, but once in a while to learn about the past, it kind of gives you an edge, and the better understanding of your music, the performance that you want to do.

Part III   Learning From the Outside

The Music Learning Profiles Project

This section explores different themes that have emerged from analysis of the 20 flash studies above. As mentioned in Part I, as the number of flash studies grows, so too will the themes and insights that emerge from them. The discussion of themes in this section by no means represents all possible experiences and commonalities among musicians who have learned music primarily outside of school-based contexts. Nevertheless, it is worthwhile to examine some emergent themes from the flash studies included in this book. Over time, we and/or others may posit a theory or theories of music learning based on what we learn from the flash studies, but at this point it is too soon to propose such a theory.

Findings discussed in this section are organized according to the following themes:

- Hybridized learning (mixture of formal, informal, etc.)
- Intentionality
- Learning by doing
- Mentorship
- Epiphany moments
- Value and meaning of music and musicking
- Passing it on
- Rejection of or opposition to school music education
- DIY and being self-taught
- Civic and cultural influence

Additional themes arose throughout the process of analysis. A complete list of themes, including some yet to be explored, appears in Appendix B in this document.

Hybridized Learning

As discussed in Section 1 of this book, we would emphasize that the dichotomy sometimes imagined and implied between formal and informal learning practices is misleading. As Green (2002) and Folkestad (2006) have done, we urge readers to consider formalness on a continuum that also includes facilitated, non-formal learning. The term 'informal learning' tends necessarily to connote a lack of formality; however, there is much discipline and rigor to informal learning practices. We argue that the different formalities are not the same as the absence of formality. With that in mind, research participants described valuable music learning experiences from both inside and outside of school contexts—hybridized learning experiences (Smith, 2013a). Although most of the flash study participants' musical learning happened outside of schools and music lessons, several participants also participated in school-based music ensembles and/or took private lessons. Gavin recalled taking a series of guitar lessons "to learn the mechanics of fingerpicking" and a handful of vocal lessons to understand better the workings of his voice. Jacqueline never had a regular guitar teacher, but instead took one-off or occasional lessons with local musicians and teachers. Piano player Rod reported that he had "very good piano teachers" who taught him "traditional classical music."

Several flash study participants were also involved in school-based music experiences. Jacqueline formed rock bands at school, and The Twilite Tone participated in school music programs and marching band programs. Tone explained that his participation in these ensembles was influential in his musical development:

> My education in the marching band situation was vast, man, because not only was I learning music, how to play an instrument, but I was learning how to have workability, in motion . . . it's like we're moving and we're creating dance and sequences and having to keep count. It's a certain amount of discipline, but it's a certain amount of freedom that you have to have within that.

Jacqueline explained that she has taken lessons in "music theory, scales, chords, all of that" but is teaching herself to improve her sight-reading. In college, Tiny found courses for developing her burgeoning MC skills, while in high school, Ray incorporated his gospel roots and the sounds of the church in his school choir. Learning in more traditional institutional settings formed part of these musicians' approaches to learning, but (crucially) on their own terms.

Intentionality

Participants in the MLPP demonstrated 'intentionality' (Anscombe, 2000; Lincoln and Guba, 1985; Searle, 1983, 1997, 1998; Schwandt, 2007) in their statements, actions, ways of seeing their environs, those with whom they interact, and in their self-perceptions. Anscombe (2000) described intention as a single phenomenon observable in human expressions (e.g., I intend to be a musician), actions (e.g., I make music), and explanations of actions (e.g., I make music because . . .). The latter category represents a coupling of expression and action (Anscombe, 2000) and is most akin to our understanding of intentionality.

Searle (1983) noted that intention and intentionality do not necessarily go hand in hand. In other words, one might intend without intentionality. The "directedness" of intent represents a hallmark of intentionality (3). The authors found Anscombe's (2000) coupling of action and expression, and the directedness of intentionality identified by Searle (1983), to be particularly revealing in our deliberations of participant expressions, actions, and reflections. Intentionality exists as part of the weft and warp of 'background' forces, including existing traditions, established practices, accepted conventions, and collective belief systems (Searle, 1983, 1997).

Regelski (2002, 2013) has applied Searle's work to essential questions regarding the value, function, and de facto practices of contemporary music education. Regelski (2013, 8) described 'background' as "the attitudes, dispositions, values, social institutions, paradigms, and practices that shape who we are, what we conceive and value, and what we can create." Pignato (2013) noted that individuals engage those background forces in ongoing reconciliations, locating intentionality "at the nexus of inner mental processes and outward engagement of the world" (9). The expressed intentions of the MLPP participants underscore the degrees to which they function as motivated actors (Tilly, 1990), purposefully curating identities while reflecting on, engaging with, and setting themselves in opposition to the prevailing 'background' (Searle, 1983, 1997) contexts in which they live, work, and create. For example, the comments of hip-hop producer Anthony 'The Twilite Tone' Khan:

> So as I, as a kid as I rebelled against it, we circle back, don't we? We circle back to those things we rebelled against and look at them in a different context . . . Now I see it with great value. I'm glad. I'm glad that I had that as an institution to rebel against. I'm glad I rebelled and I'm appreciative that I can see that right now, at this moment of time.

Similarly, Intikana Kekoiea asserted that "the one question we're all trying to answer is 'Who am I?' 'Who am I?' 'Why am I?' 'Why am I who I am?' 'Do I matter?' 'Who have I been?' 'Where do I come from?'" Amia 'Tiny' Jackson's explanation of how she got started rapping reveals a similar outlook:

> That's basically how I started rapping; just from seeing things [going on in her home]. You know, I didn't really have any other outlets to

express what I was feeling, so I did it by rapping. That's how I started. I wanted to rap about their [adult family relations] problems to let them know, "I understand what y'all talking about." They used to come and just gossip, like, from watching people be abused, they come in talking about being cheated on. That's what I rapped about for a lot of my life. It's about what I seen and how the other females were being treated for a very long time.

Shana Falana, spoke of being 'defiant' throughout her musical development, in regard to a childhood piano teacher's lessons, in opposition to a patriarchal bandleader, and in response to music business expectations often foisted upon female musicians.

Thus, we have found the intentionality with which participants speak about their music lives remarkable. The same intentionality informs their navigation of richly complex social lives at once bound and subject to their music making.

Learning by Doing

A preference for learning by 'doing' (as opposed to learning through being taught) was a recurring theme, reflecting the 'informal' learning practices of musicians identified by Green (2001), also described as "natural" (Green, 2008a, 42), a notion supported by Stålhammar (2003) and resonating with Bamberger's (1978, 173) concept of "intuitive musical knowing." (As we noted earlier, these 'informal' learning practices are helpfully understood as components of self-directed, hybridized learning approaches.) Jacqueline, for instance, learned guitar largely by "watching guitar lesson videos on YouTube, jamming alone and messing around." Gavin felt strongly that "being fired is the best educational experience you'll get—every time I get fired from something, I need to get better at something else." Jacquelyn found that "you learn everything on the job," while Sean described the practical knowledge acquired from "learning on the bandstand." Sean used the phrase 'learning on the bandstand' to describe his real-world music education experience. He explained that to learn on the bandstand was efficient because "it doesn't willfully ignore the skills that might be most germane to a career in hip-hop such as the ability to rap on beat, interact with a crowd and prepare music that is mixed properly for stage performance." From across the traditions inhabited by these musicians, most emphasized the importance of learning music in and through non-written forms, also typical of 'natural', 'intuitive', and informal modes of learning. Rod emphasized the importance of ear training and listening (on the radio) to as many popular songs as possible. Rod emphasized the on-the-job nature of learning his craft, saying that "the good thing about what I do is that I do get to play every day . . . just from doing that, you get better, and you can try all sorts of different things out."

The ethos of 'learning by doing' was especially evident in the of the experiences of the profiled hip-hop artists. Through the process of 'street battling', these artists honed their craft. The Twilight Tone described the process of battling and said it "helped to influence and to inspire the kind of music I make." Intikana explained the importance of battling in the development of his craft, but also in the development of a "warrior spirit":

> Initially, [my rhymes] were just for me, maybe for my very close group of friends until, eventually, I got heavily into battling. Battling that's when in school, especially in high school, it was very prevalent, if anyone heard you rap it wasn't like you could just rap and make a song, it was like people were knocking on your door, while you were in class, waiting for you to come out so they could battle you. So, it was a very competitive atmosphere but it was also a chance to always be on your toes. It was . . . it was in many ways, exciting, like a warrior spirit. I learned a lot from those experiences and then eventually I had the opportunity to go to college, which I was very hesitant to initially, I didn't want to.

The benefits of such 'constructivist' learning (see e.g., Custodero, 2010) need to be explored further, we argue, shedding light on a medium of learning through doing and learning as knowing.

Mentorship

Another consistent theme throughout the analyzed flash studies is that of mentorship experiences for the musicians, overlapping with the hybridized learning described above. Even those who described themselves as 'self-taught' also described some sort of mentorship experience where an older, more experienced musician showed them the tricks of the trade. Due to limitations and access to 'master' musicians, learners 'on the outside' often do their learning quite differently from school learners. Thus, they ascribe "pedagogic authority" (Bourdieu and Passeron, 1977, 19) to a range of role models who are excluded from much discourse in mainstream music education.

The Twilight Tone recalled having multiple mentors, or "big brothers," functioning like masters to Tone's apprentice. Tone explained, "I had big brothers along the way that said, 'Hey man, do you know about this? Do you know about that?'" For Amia 'Tiny' Jackson, her family provided formidable role models in her life. Tiny explained, "I somewhat followed my aunt, she rapped too and is really good; very lyrical, nasty. Like, I'm good but she's, I'll say she's great; yeah, she's awesome."

Truth Universal's neighborhood buddies functioned as mentors for Truth by showing him how to make beats on the early versions of the Boss Dr. Rhythm and then scratch old records over the drum machine. Sean cited some key mentor–mentee relationships with older, more experienced musicians in the Minneapolis area as being a key element of his music education. Sean credits much of his growth as a musician to the fact that he was able to learn the ropes from more veteran musicians. The mentoring approaches that seem to pervade learning practices need closer investigation to establish challenges and merits.

Epiphany Moments

Several flash study participants described epiphany moments (Pignato, 2013) as an important part of their musical learning experience. Andy recalled having an epiphany moment the day that Jimi Hendrix died, which caused him to quit the football team and focus on music. Gavin described how hearing a one-eyed fisherman singing sublimely in a pub in rural Ireland led him to quit electronic music to pursue expression of purity and truth with his own voice as a folk singer. Intikana described an experience in his university's library as a pivotal moment for him.

> I was like, "wow, I wonder what they have on Puerto Rico, here." . . . I couldn't find nothing on Taino. I couldn't find nothing on my ancestors. It tripped me out because it made me think that we didn't have a history, no culture, no music. Here I was at college and, like, I didn't have a history.

These epiphany moments are akin to 'critical incidents' (e.g. Burnard, 2012), and key to understanding and nurturing people's being and becoming, as musicians and community members.

Value and Meaning of Music and Musicking

The value and meaning of music comprised a theme across the flash study profiles, significant perhaps because of challenges these musicians' statements may pose to norms and assumptions in school music education. Jacquelyn, for example, offered a critique to pervading neoliberal assumptions that inform so much music education (Parkinson, 2014; Parkinson and Smith, 2015), especially at college level:

> The arts have a value above and beyond that [making money], really, which is immeasurable . . . and it goes beyond each individual art as

well . . . Music is music, at the end of the day—why do we have to keep defining it in other terms, and justifying it by other value systems?

DeVeor commented on how narrow notions of success in music and of music making can fail to include the plethora of music making experiences that are happening everywhere: "When we see the bucket players on the street or the kids drumming on the tables, that should be viewed as a music education experience. They shouldn't be devalued. That should be significant, you know?" Gavin was hesitant to self-define as 'professional', despite broad, deep skillsets, due to an uneasiness around his impression that professionalism too often implies 'corporate' or commodification. He takes pride in functioning outside of the mainstream music industry, saying that "I often deliberately do things with the minimum 'professionalism', but the maximum possible artistic output."

Passing It On

Just as many of the profiled musicians received help along the way from a mentor, they were in turn eager to 'pass it on' to the next generation of musicians. Gavin shared that he is keen to help people, and to respond to anyone who asks questions or seeks guidance, leaving a legacy of enabling other artists. Ray's work as a musician and teacher and his development of the Center for Gospel Arts exemplify his working with students to promote and perpetuate the tradition of gospel music. In Ray's words, "once a mentor discovers someone has some potential, they invest in them. And then you have a musician who plays very well, but who may have never stepped in an academic setting."

Jacqueline gave voluntary guitar lessons at her old secondary school, where she "showed some of the students how to shred a bit," and has recorded YouTube instructional videos in hopes of sharing some of what she has learned. Neville has adopted a few mentees—some local and some from across the globe. Neville explained:

Generally, I try to mentor them and we figure out things together, like what makes melodies memorable and share back and forth. I've even given workshops all the way in Australia on songwriting; just trying to share all the principles I learned 'outside' school . . . I haven't heard of any formal songwriting classes that teach that.

JB recalled providing assistance to one of today's most well-known multi-selfers: Jacob Collier. JB helped Jacob learn how to do the video editing for multi-selfing videos, and now Jacob has over 13 million YouTube views and has won multiple Grammy awards. JB shared, "I feel very lucky to have that early connection with him."

Rejection of or Opposition to School Music Education

> Honestly, what I would do, I would send them, well, I wouldn't send them to a school, hell no! Y'all ain't gonna learn how to do hip hop in a school. I would send them to a . . . I'm looking for the proper word. I would send them to a damaged neighborhood and tell them write about what they see. I think that's the first step to hip-hop.
>
> —Amia 'Tiny' Jackson

Gavin also expressed disdain for and distrust of the educational system, in his case in the UK, saying that "every experience I've ever had in an institution has been appalling . . . I am completely DIY, I don't believe in academic education—it's just a good way to make money for a lot of people." Reflecting on first learning the guitar, Andy recalled that there was little connection between the music that he was interested in playing and the music ensembles at his school, stating, "I had nothing to do with any formal music program, school music or private lessons after the age of 11." Similarly, Anthony 'The Twilite Zone' Khan recalled that

> I wanted to create music. I didn't want to be in the marching band anymore . . . it actually inspired me to want to rebel against convention and structure . . . think outside of the lines or to color outside of the lines.

Jacqueline described music in compulsory education to be "boxing people in, rather than letting them free to be creative." Ray found that at the collegiate level, many of his musical skills were not "honored by the institution of university music schools." This sentiment was echoed by Neville, who explained that at his university, the "faculty frowned on that 'outside' stuff," despite the fact that the very music being studied 'inside' arose 'outside' the walls of brick and mortar institutions.

For several hip-hop artists profiled, in-school music seemed at odds with the skills necessary to learn their craft. Hip-hop artist Truth stated, "true artistry does not come from a blueprint where students with As have any real skills." Similarly, Intikana expressed feeling apart from, or othered by, institutional learning. This rejection of school music education could also be found in the experiences of several musicians who took traditional piano lessons. Shana reflected on her experiences with traditional piano lessons and stated:

> I took piano lessons when I was a little girl, maybe around seven. That was the last time I tried to read sheet music. I remember my piano teacher, I would learn the song but I would make changes to it. I would rewrite some of the material and my teacher, well, let's say my teacher really frowned upon that [chuckles]. So I stopped taking piano lessons because I felt like it wasn't fun.

Andy initially had a good experience with a piano teacher who taught him how to play Beatles songs. However, after switching to a more traditional piano teacher at his father's request, Andy quickly lost interest and quit taking piano lessons.

DIY and Being Self-Taught

Perhaps in response to the previously discussed opposition to school-based music, the majority of musicians profiled expressed that they were 'self-taught' (see above for how this notion also intersects with the hybridized learning and mentoring experiences). Gavin explained, "I am self-taught in every regard," and expressed a deep sense of pride and empowerment at being an independently functioning musician, drawing heavily on the DIY punk ethos (Gordon, 2012).

Reflecting on first learning the guitar, Andy explained, "I sort of prided myself on this idea of being self-taught and I wanted to follow the way that I thought my heroes had learned music, being self-taught."

Jacqueline explained that she learned guitar largely by "watching guitar lesson videos on YouTube, jamming alone and messing around." Shana described teaching herself "in private where I would just mimic what I was hearing, picking the notes out by ear. I always had a good ear so I could pick the notes out and learn what I wanted." Similarly, Neville described the radio as his primary influence. "The radio was my best friend. I would sing along to all kinds of music. If anything was my teacher, it was that. There was something intuitive about listening and emulating what I heard." Ray also learned from the radio through imitation, often connecting sounds from the radio to his piano playing style.

Intikana exemplified learning by doing, and explained "I never really had somebody teach me skills, how to do things . . . . I just taught myself." Similarly, hip-hop artist Tiny explained "I never really sat down with somebody, like 'you're gonna do this, this, this, and that.' I did it myself, I wrote raps."

Civic and Cultural Influence

Cities and cultural communities often played roles in the musical development of the profiled artists. This was most notable in the lives of hip-hop artists and their connections to New York City. Intikana grew up in the Bronx, the geographic location most frequently associated with the birth of hip-hop culture, as did DeVeor. Growing up in the epicenter of the hip-hop movement affected how DeVeor felt about participating in school music ensembles. She explained,

> Honestly, even if there was good music programs in school [sic], I wouldn't have been involved because my high school years coincided with the start of hip-hop and hip-hop didn't stress playing instruments, so I didn't bother with playing music in school.

The prevalence of hip-hop in New York City also influenced Amia 'Tiny' Jackson, who wrote rhymes and kept a notebook of rap lyrics in her Brooklyn, New York apartment. Tiny explained, "That's basically how I started rapping; just from seeing things and having nothing else to do but write; because that's what everybody else was doing."

The Twilite Tone drew influences from the dance music culture of his native Chicago. Dancing in Chicago, as in other major US cities during the '70s and '80s, happened in clubs but also on the street as young dancers joined crews and danced in competitive battles (Chang, 2005; Katz, 2012). The creative culture in San Francisco was a big influence on Shana Falana, who explained, "Everybody was sort of exploring, experimenting, and we were all supporting each other and it was just a great time to, to play with other people and to experiment with different sounds." Neville, who was born in St. Thomas, a US Virgin Island, and Truth Universal, a native Trinidadian, both referenced the cultural influences around them growing up. Neville spoke of his connection to music from an early age with drums and piano, while Truth referenced the blending of African, Caribbean, jazz, second line, soca, calypso, reggae, funk, and R&B music all around him during his youth. This civic and cultural influence can also be see in Riduan's passion for Malay drumming, which he learned as a boy in Singapore.

Implications and Applications

This stage of the project, solidified here in book form, is really its genesis. The flash studies captured in the MLPP are much more than anecdotes about people's musics and practices. The MLPP captures lived learning experiences in increasingly international contexts. These perspectives and stories are important in that they help to preserve and promote musical traditions and experiences. They can also serve to help professional and scholarly communities glean and apply insights that can help shape their futures. The potential of the MLPP is delimited by the diversity of the flash studies and by the insights of researchers and readers.

During our early work on the MLPP, we considered deriving from the themes an evolving, overarching theoretical framework regarding 'outside' music learning practices. We soon realized, however, that such a framework might serve, moreover, to overlook understandings and distilled, contextualized knowings that this project affords others who engage with it. Music teaching and learning are not static processes. They are human, dynamic, and organic. They require interaction, social dynamics, and adaptable responsiveness. We hope that the MLPP benefits from the marinating effects of time and input from diverse contributors. The MLPP allows for and encourages contingent, iterative learning theories to emerge.

Musical stories that include learning, knowing, telling, and transmission exist in many forms and contexts. They belong to no field in particular, but among various fields, independently and at their intersections. As we noted in Part I, these include ethnomusicology, popular music studies, and music education. The music education contexts can include primary, secondary, tertiary, and community contexts. The spaces may be both physical and/or online, and may include private tuition. The MLPP captures the perspectives of many musicians whose stories can speak to learners, scholars, and practitioners in each of these environments. The MLPP is an organic, dynamic project with potential to present implications into the future. Important to this iterative process is that implications and pursuant applications should, we anticipate, lead to further implications and more applications. The conclusions and suggestions below are, therefore, far from exhaustive.

Ethnomusicology, Popular Music Studies, and Music Learning

The MLPP speaks to multi- and inter-disciplinary study, for instance in the closely related fields of ethnomusicology and popular music studies. Popular music studies is situated across disciplines, including ethnomusicology, which in turn often embraces popular music studies. The MLPP, through short, rich, robust flash study analyses, helps to bring into focus the potential to explore an eclectic breadth of musicalities. The MLPP offers to help break down barriers and their implicit institutionalized disciplinary power structures as it encourages those in institutionalized contexts to permit and incorporate a range of musicalities, creativities, and musickings. As scholars learn more from this project—especially its planned database—about how music is learned, made, and experienced in diverse contexts, they (and we) will be able to apply that knowledge in new ways.

Thorough consideration of the pedagogical implications of particular artists' stories regarding their music learning backgrounds in (non-)institutionalized settings (of course, all settings are in their own ways institutionalized), could benefit from combined perspectives in music education, popular music studies, and ethnomusicology. By cross-fertilizing ideas, methods and practices, the perspectives and understandings hybridize, becoming richer. We understand this to be what Harrison, Mackinlay, and Pettan (2010) referred to as "applied ethnomusicology." Music educators, in particular, may find the applied ethnomusicological approaches enriching in their discussion of sociocultural aspects of musical learning practices. We suggest that the field of music education is positioned to gain especially from the convergence of ethnomusicological considerations in pedagogical contexts.

Music Education

The themes presented above can, we hope, help guide, steer, and inform the work of colleagues in the music education profession. If it is true that there is an aggregate of beneficial teaching and learning approaches that recur in the MLPP data, then it would behoove those in the music education profession to acknowledge and seek to apply some of these practices as appropriate. The MLPP, we argue, helps to promote a more ethical pedagogical approach because its insights can be incorporated by music educators striving to provide relevant, salient experiences for their students, in light of and in spite of broader sociopolitical environments that enable and constrain their work. We acknowledge that our colleagues in the music education profession are frequently not averse to such ideas, nor unaware of them. Our aim is to highlight possible additions to the palette of music education experiences. As Froehlich (2007, 65) asserted, music teachers' reflections

> have practical value if they help each teacher to understand . . . where school music fits into the larger scheme of education as a social mandate, and the specifics of school politics created by daily interactions with colleagues and administrative superiors.

Mentorship is a case in point. While MLPP participants discussed their musical mentors at length, it is rare to find mentoring as a standard practice in school music education contexts, outside of master–apprentice models still common to much conservatory training. Scholars in the music education profession might explore and seek to implement more research on mentorship; web developers could look to promote digital spaces for mentorship. Mentors may share with one another in a process of professional development. The more we explore these topics, the more the profession can benefit and progress towards more diverse, context-relevant, and functional pedagogies.

While practitioners are busy diligently planning and teaching, they may unwittingly and unintentionally be being guided by what Froehlich and Smith (2017, 102) refer to as a "hidden curriculum." The musics and associated practices and assumptions that practitioners employ in their practice can serve to limit, constrain, and frame music learning—purveying what Green (2008b, 246) refers to as particular "delineated musical meaning." A practitioner who reads through the flash studies might thus start to develop a more eclectic musical and music-teaching palate.

This can be a dangerous process, particularly when one considers how narrow in scope systemized music education can be. There are "deep-seated problems with what is considered valued knowledge by those who hold the power to make sociopolitical and educational decisions" (Froehlich, 2007, 96). Practitioners often emerge from a culture of promotion and propagation, often cyclical and culturally exclusive. The more that practitioners are informed by diversity and the true lived experiences of musicians from all backgrounds—including their students and the students' families and communities—the more likely they are to apply this to knowledge giving, sharing, and creation.

A music education professor teaching undergraduates, for example, might encourage their students to explore the MLPP for learning styles and habits that are often overlooked in their teacher manuals, prior classes, or other resources and materials. A professor of a methods class, for instance, might ask students to read through the MLPP and guide a discussion through facilitated questions such as: How might an elementary school music teacher apply learning from two or three MLPP flash studies in a series of 3rd-grade hip-hop lessons? How might a professional musician operate as a mentor in middle school band settings? How might high school students find ways to promote what they know to their peers, to help expand their high school music program beyond those currently enrolled?

A music education mentor of, e.g., graduate student teachers, might encourage a mentee to sort through the digital database of the MLPP and have the students design a series of lesson plans around the musical practices of one particular pedagogical style. These could then be taught in a series of micro lessons in an iterative process of teaching, feedback, and reflection. Later on, that same music education professor might ask her graduate students to write their own flash studies of musicians known to them and relate them to some in the repository, finding commonalities, differences, and other points of interest, for instance indexing and annotating them. Those same graduate students might harness what they have learned about musical learning from the MLPP in teaching virtually through video conference to help students in underserved populations learn and understand more about particular musical and cultural heritages—including their own. These students could then work with a local music educator to join her multicultural music orchestra class in a community concert to celebrate cultures often overlooked by school music traditions.

We hope that music educators will be inspired and empowered by the richness of music learning presented in and anticipated by the MLPP. We seek not to prescribe ways in which music education communities or individuals should digest or put into practice our work. These should be local decisions, up to the individuals who connect with their students, and contingent upon practicable music teaching and learning applications in particular contexts.

Diversity, Inclusion, and Affirmation

Contemporary musics are created, performed, and understood within disparate cultural, social, geographic, and economic contexts. Although connections between such contexts have led to greater understandings and the popularization of hybrid musical forms (Hebert, 2009), bridges between those cultural contexts and schooling often remain under-supported. The MLPP can function as a bridge. We know that musical movements emerge from situated cultural places (Hebdige, 1979), and from 'poietic' spaces (Nattiez, 1990). Such locales differ considerably from one another and from the spaces available to aspiring musicians in school contexts.

Ethnomusicologists are often committed to exploring and understanding diverse musics and musicking. Institutionalized school music education, on the other hand, tends—consciously or not—to promote a thin slice of the world's musics, through acts of bias and cultural oppression. The occasional multicultural musics that do appear in school music are often served up as asides, taking place in music appreciation classes, tokenistic crowd-pleasing concert pieces, or interdisciplinary, governmentally mandated cultural heritage celebrations. There thus exists an otherizing or othering effect, whereby diverse musics can be relegated to the outside, ostracized from what is considered appropriate school music.

Through the blending of disciplines and fields (music education, popular music studies, and ethnomusicology), the MLPP aims to help democratize the field of music education. It liberates ideas, empowers voices, and disrupts conventional thinking. It has been widely documented that in many (although by no means all) international contexts, music education in K–12 schools appears to be losing the battle with twenty-first century students on cultural relevancy merits (Green, 2002; Harrop-Allin, 2011; Kratus, 2007; Marsh, 2011; Mok, 2011; Pitts, 2011; Preston, 2013; Williams, 2011). Hopefully the MLPP can influence the next generation of music educators to effect change in K–12 settings. Constant rethinking, reshaping, and evaluating is the only way school music can become and remain relevant to, and in the eyes of, the younger generation whom it serves.

The MLPP, through presentation of diverse case studies of music making and learning, helps educators to consider and conceptualize greater levels of musical equity for the contexts in which they work. This includes bringing forward marginalized pedagogical and musical styles. It implicates scholars, practitioners, students, publishers, free press enthusiasts, online social media resource sharers, maker-space developers, and more. The MLPP exists at the center, the fringes, and beyond the periphery of current music education discourse. The more we, as a total profession, value a wider, more inclusive range of musical traditions, the more we all can be poised to benefit.

We caution against the reification of musics, works, practices, and knowledges. There would be too great an irony in this work perpetuating further canonizing of practices, in the very epistemological mode that we seek to challenge. We hope that as the MLPP unfolds and readers explore and celebrate musically rich diversities, people can also come to realize their similarities. We also expect that we can learn a great deal about our diversities and the many ways in which our differences can inform us. Understanding and celebrating our similarities and our differences can hopefully lead to the nexus of a new and perpetually renewing music education. The publication of this book feels timely, for at no point in the authors' lives has it seemed more important to emphasize, cherish, and celebrate diversity, and to draw attention to the richness, vibrancy, and vitality of musicking (being human) in all its messy, real, political, and personal glory. We never expected that standing up for these things would or even could appear radical. It now feels obligatory, and of critical importance.

In Summary

It is worth recalling that, more than 20 years ago, Björnberg noted:

> The open, informal and collective learning processes at work in the everyday practices of many popular music styles differ in several respects from those of institutional education. To what extent and how such 'alternative' learning processes can be used (and to what extent they are even necessary) in teaching popular music within music education institutions remains an urgent question.

(1993, 76)

The urgency of this issue remains. We intend to use data gathered by the MLPP in stimulating this ongoing discussion regarding what constitutes music learning, and to construct theoretical frameworks that explain and explore learning practices and styles of musicians. We hope, at the very least, that the MLPP provides a platform for dialogue about music learning habits and practices often overlooked and marginalized. Our plans for the MLPP are ambitious, and to date the MLPP has received no institutional or external funding. The authors hope that the publication of this book serves to validate our nascent project, thus strengthening future applications for funding to pursue this research (no grant applications have been made to date in connection with this work).

The artists featured in the flash study analyses above exemplify lives dedicated to what Froehlich and Smith (2017, 129) described as "voluntary immersion in a music-making culture." For some this has meant brushes with formal(ized) (e.g., school) music education experiences. For others, it has not. For all, though, there is a recognition that the active pursuit of music is essential to creating and living a life. How these people learn, what they learn, and what they believe to be important for others to learn in and through music, could inform music teachers' work in several ways. These could include educators doing the following:

- Looking for evidence of and potential for an eclectic breadth of musicalities among students;
- Incorporating learning and music-making approaches from more diverse musicking traditions into school music activities;
- Valuing a wider, more inclusive range of musical traditions;
- Permitting and incorporating a range of musicalities, creativities, and musicking in the school music classroom.

The MLPP aims thus to help weave closer together the interconnected fields of music education and ethnomusicology. Students and academics from each can learn from one another's approaches and perspectives, and we hope that the MLPP will facilitate cross-fertilization of ideas, methods, and practices. Constant rethinking, reshaping, and evaluating are essential for school music to become relevant to the younger generation whom it aims to serve.

As Froehlich and Smith (2017, 129) wrote, music "has the advantage of being integral to our people's lives outside of the school environment." With music being thus 'integral', school (and college) music educators (and their administrators) have an ethical responsibility to facilitate and recognize meaningful, valuable education in music for all students. Exactly what form(s) this takes will necessarily vary from context to context. Hopefully educators will feel inspired and empowered by the richness of music learning presented in the flash study analyses—both individually and in aggregate—to work to conceive and help students to achieve appropriate and relevant music education goals, "developing understanding, insightfulness, qualities of mind" (Swanwick, 1988, 36).

Invitation to Contribute

Essentially, the MLPP has two functions. First, it tells the stories of musicians so that musicians, scholars, and educators might consider avenues towards engaging newer and broader learnerships through those practices. It also aims to offer an accessible publication platform for contributors, including early-stage scholars, practitioners, and seasoned professionals. We hope that this invitation will lead to thousands of flash studies that enrich and diversify the repository. Scholars of all backgrounds are welcome to the MLPP. All ways of learning and teaching are valued. The more we can share, the more we can learn. If the MLPP can do anything for our musical heritages and cultures, it is to tell and preserve some of the many stories that constitute them. We invite you to join the Music Learning Profiles Project. Information regarding the MLPP and instructions for submitting flash study analyses for consideration and inclusion in the MLPP Flash Study repository can be found at mlppflashstudies.org.

Appendix A
Interview Protocol Master

Overarching Question

What are relevant training, prior experiences, musical practices, and belief systems of each of the participants?

Interview Protocol

1. Describe what you do.
2. How long have you been doing it (rapping, singing, producing, etc.)?
3. How did you get started?
4. What were the necessary skills, abilities, and knowledge to play, rap, rhyme, spin, produce, sing, work equipment, etc.?
5. How did you acquire those skills, abilities, and knowledge?
6. Did you have any guidance, any help, or teachers of any sort?
7. Tell me more about your education, any important educational experiences related to (hip-hop, gospel, EDM), any formal training in music? If so, describe your training or any other education you would like to tell me about? What about your formal education? Did your formal education relate in any way to your work in . . .?
8. Has/does that background inform or relate to your present work?
9. Identify the prior experiences and/or education you think most influential on your abilities.
10. Is there anything else about your educational background, training, or prior experiences that informs your work that we haven't covered?
11. Where does someone go, what do they do, if they want to learn how to . . . or develop skills as . . .?
12. Have you helped, taught, or mentored a younger . . .?
13. Does one generation relate to another? How does the practice continue? Does it get passed on in any way?

Appendix B
Themes Used in Coding Flash Studies

- Adversity
- Civic influence
- Creativities
- DIY and being self-taught
- Entrepreneurialism
- Epiphany moments
- Fringes of celebrity
- Hybridized learning (mixture of formal, informal, etc.)
- Identities
- Intentionality
- Learning by doing
- Mentorship
- Passing it on
- Rejection of or opposition to school music education
- Value and meaning of music and musicking

Bibliography

Allsup, Randall E. 2010. Choosing music literature. In *Critical issues in music education: Contemporary theory and practice*, edited by Harold F. Abeles and Lori A. Custodero, 215–35. New York: Oxford University Press.

———. 2016. *Remixing the classroom: Toward an open philosophy of music education*. Bloomington: Indiana University Press.

Anscombe, Gertrude E. M. 2000. *Intention*. Cambridge: Harvard University Press.

Audubert, Philippe, Gaby Bizien, Louis Chrétiennot, Bertrand Dupouy, Thierry Duval, Thibeault Krzewina, Hervé Parent, François Rivac, and Marc Touché. 2015. *Learning and teaching popular music: Sharing experiences from France*. Translated by P. Moseley. Paris: RPM Editions.

Azzara, Christopher. 2011. *TedxRochester*. http://tedxtalks.ted.com/video/TEDxRochester-Christopher-Azzar;search%3Achristopherazzara

Bamberger, Jeanne. 1978. Intuitive and formal musical knowing: Parables of cognitive dissonance. In *The arts, cognition and basic skills*, edited by Stanley S. Madeja, 173–206. St. Louis, LA: Cemrel.

Barrett, Margaret S. 2011. Towards a cultural psychology of music education. In *A cultural psychology of music education*, edited by Margaret S. Barrett, 1–16. Oxford: Oxford University Press.

Becker, Howard S. 1973. *Outsiders: Studies in the sociology of deviance*. New York: The Free Press.

Benedict, Cathy. 2010. Methods and approaches. In *Critical issues in music education: Contemporary theory and practice*, edited by Harold F. Abeles and Lori A. Custodero, 143–66. New York: Oxford University Press.

Bennett, H. Stith. 1980. *On becoming a rock musician*. Amherst, MA: University of Massachusetts Press.

Bennett, Toby. 2015. *Learning the music business evaluating the 'vocational turn' in music industry education*. London: UK Music.

Berger, Harris M. 1999. *Metal, rock, and jazz: Perception and the phenomenology of musical experience*. Middletown, CT: Wesleyan University Press.

Berger, Peter L., and Thomas Luckmann. 1967. *The social construction of reality: A treatise in the sociology of knowledge*. New York: Anchor Books.

Björnberg, Alf. 1993. Teach you to rock? Popular music in the university music department. *Popular Music* 12: 69–77.

Bourdieu, Pierre. 2005. *The social structures of the economy*. Cambridge, UK: Polity Press.

Bourdieu, Pierre, and J. C. Passeron. 1977. *Reproduction in education, society and culture*. London, UK: Sage Publications.

Bull, Anna. 2016. El Sistema as a bourgeois social project: Class, gender, and Victorian values. *Action, Criticism, and Theory for Music Education* 15 (1): 120–53.

Burnard, Pamela. 2012. *Musical creativities in practice*. Oxford: Oxford University Press.

Campbell, Patricia S. 1995. Of garage bands and song-getting: The musical development of young rock musicians. *Research Studies in Music Education* 4 (1): 12–20.

———. 2011. Musical enculturation: Sociocultural meanings and influences of children's experiences in and through music. In *A cultural psychology of music education*, edited by Margaret S. Barrett, 61–82. Oxford: Oxford University Press.

Chang, Jeff. 2005. *Can't stop, won't stop: A history of the hip hop generation*. New York: MacMillan.

Church, Terry. 2010. "Black history month: Jesse Saunders and house music." *Beatport News*. http://news.beatport.com/blog/2010/02/09/black-history-jesse-saunders-and-house-music/

Cremata, R. and B. Powell. 2017. Online music collaboration project: Digitally mediated, deterritorialized music education. *International Journal of Music Education* 35 (2): 302–15.

Creswell, John W. 2007. *Qualitative inquiry and research design: Choosing among five approaches*. London: Sage Publications.

Custodero, Lori A. 2010. Music learning and musical development. In *Critical issues in music education: Contemporary theory and practice*, edited by Harold F. Abeles and Lori A. Custodero, 113–42. New York: Oxford University Press.

Dewey, John. 1916. *Essays in experimental logic*. Chicago, IL: University of Chicago.

———. (1938) 2007. *Experience and education*. London: Simon and Schuster.

Feleppa, Robert. 1986. Emics, etics, and social objectivity. *Current Anthropology*: 243–55.

Folkestad, Göran. 2006. "Formal and informal learning situations or practices vs formal and informal ways of learning." *British Journal of Music Education*. 23. 135–45. 10.1017/S0265051706006887.

Froehlich, Hildegard C. 2007. *Sociology for music teachers: Perspectives for practice*. Upper Saddle River, NJ: Prentice Hall.

Froehlich, Hildegard C., and Gareth D. Smith. 2017. *Sociology for music teachers: Practical applications*. New York: Routledge.

Garfield, Joey. 2002. *Breath control: The history of the human beat box*. [Documentary film]. Brooklyn, NY: Ghost Robot Productions.

Goble, Scott. 2010. Nationalism in United States music education during World War II. *Journal of Historical Research in Music Education* 30: 103–17.

Gordon, Alistair. 2012. Building recording studios while Bradford burned. In *Punkademis: The basement show in the ivory tower*, edited by Zack Furness, 105–24. Brooklyn, NY: Minor Compositions.

Green, Lucy. 2002. *How popular musicians learn: A way ahead for music education*. Aldershot, UK: Ashgate.

———. 2008a. *Music, informal learning and the school: A new classroom pedagogy*. Aldershot, UK: Ashgate.

———. 2008b. *Music on deaf ears: Music, ideology, education*. Manchester: Manchester University Press.

———. 2011. Introduction. In *Learning, teaching, and musical identity: Voices across cultures*, edited by Lucy Green, 1–19. Bloomington: Indiana University Press.

Harrison, Klisala, Elizabeth Mackinlay, and Svanibor Pettan. 2010. *Applied ethnomusicology: Historical and contemporary approaches*. Newcastle Upon Tyne, UK: Cambridge Scholars Publishing.

Harrop-Allin, Susan. 2011. Playing with Barbie: Exploring South African township children's games as resources for pedagogy. In *Learning, teaching, and musical identity: Voices across cultures*, edited by Lucy Green, 156–69. Bloomington: Indiana University Press.

Hebert, David, Joseph Abramo, and Gareth Dylan Smith. 2017. Epistemological and sociological issues in popular music education. In *The Ashgate research companion to popular music education*, edited by Gareth Dylan Smith, Zack Moir, Matt Brennan, Shara Rambarran, and Phil Kirkman. Farnham: Ashgate.

Hebdige, Dick. 1979. *Subculture: The meaning of style*. London, UK: Routledge.

Hebert, David G. 2009. Musicianship, musical identity, and meaning as embodied practice. In *Music education for changing times*, edited by Thomas A. Regelski and J. Terry Gates, 39–55. Netherlands: Springer.

Higgins, Lee. 2012. *Community music in theory and in practice*. New York: Oxford University Press.

Horsley, Stephanie. 2015. Facing the music: Pursuing social justice through music education in a neoliberal world. In *The Oxford handbook of social justice in music education*, edited by Cathy Benedict, Patrick Schmidt, Gary Spruce, and Paul Woodford, 62–77. New York: Oxford University Press.

IFPI. 2017. *IFPI-Global Music Report 2017*. www.ifpi.org/news/IFPI-GLOBAL-MUSIC-REPORT-2017. Accessed August 13, 2017.

Jenkins, Henry. 2006. *Convergence Culture: Where old and new media collide*. New York: New York University Press.

Kallio, Alexis A. 2015. Navigating (un)popular music in the classroom: Censure and censorship in an inclusive, democratic music education. Doctoral diss., Sibelius Academy of the University of the Arts, Helsinki.

———. 2017. Popular 'problems': Deviantization and teachers' curation of popular music. *International Journal of Music Education* 35 (3): 319–32.

Kaplan, Max. 1943. Beethoven or a bottle of beer? *Junior College Journal* 13: 373–5.

———. 1945. Music for community or catalogue? *Junior College Journal* 16 (September): 25.

———. 1958. *Music in the community: A report for Music in American Life Commission VIII*. Washington, DC: Music Educators National Conference.

Katz, Mark. 2012. *Groove music: The art and culture of the hip hop DJ*. New York: Oxford University Press.

Kratus, John. 2007. Music education at the tipping point. *Music Educators Journal* 94 (2): 42–8.

Lincoln, Yvonna, and Evon Guba. 1985. *Naturalistic inquiry*. Beverly Hills, CA: Sage Publications.

Lingard, Bob. 2010. Towards a sociology of pedagogies. In *The Routledge international handbook of the sociology of education*, edited by Michael W. Apple, Stephen J. Ball, and Luis A. Gandin, 167–78. Oxford: Routledge.

Mantie, Roger. 2014. Liminal or lifelong: Leisure, recreation, and the future of music education. In *Music education: Navigating the future*, edited by Clint Randles. New York: Routledge.

———. 2016. Leisure Grooves: An open letter to Charles Keil. In *The Oxford handbook of music making and leisure*, edited by R. Mantie and G. D. Smith, 621–40. New York: Oxford University Press.

Marsh, Kathryn. 2011. The permeable classroom: Learning, teaching, and musical identity in a remote Australian aboriginal homelands school. In *Learning, teaching, and musical identity: Voices across cultures*, edited by Lucy Green, 20–32. Bloomington: Indiana University Press.

McPherson, Sean. 2012. *How do you teach hip-hop the same way you learned it?* Paper presented at New York University's Show and Prove Conference, New York, NY.

Merriam, Sharan. B. 1998. *Qualitative research and case study applications in education*. San Francisco, CA: Jossey-Bass Publishers.

Moir, Zack, Bryan Powell, and Gareth D. Smith. In Press. *The Bloomsbury handbook of popular music education: Practices and perspectives*. London: Bloomsbury.

Mok, Roe-Min. 2011. Music for a post-colonial child: Theorizing Malaysian memories. In *Learning, teaching, and musical identity: Voices across cultures*, edited by Lucy Green, 73–90. Bloomington: Indiana University Press.

Morgan, David. 2008. Snowball sampling. In *The Sage encyclopedia of qualitative research methods*, edited by Lisa Given, 816–17. Thousand Oaks, CA: Sage Publications.

Nattiez, Jean-Jacques. 1990. *Music and discourse: Toward a semiology of music*. Translated by Carolyn Abbate. Princeton, NJ: Princeton University Press.

Parkinson, Tom. 2014. Values in higher popular music education. Doctoral diss., University of Reading, Reading, UK.

Parkinson, Tom, and Gareth D. Smith. 2015. Towards an epistemology of authenticity in higher popular music education. *Action, Criticism, and Theory for Music Education* 14 (1): 93–127.

Partti, Heidi. 2012. *Learning from cosmopolitan digital musicians: Identity, musicianship, and changing values in (in)formal music communities*. Helsinki: Sibelius Academy.

Pignato, Joseph M. 2013. Angelica gets the spirit out: Improvisation, epiphany and transformation. *Research Studies in Music Education* 35 (1): 25–38.

———. 2017a. Situating technology within and without music education. In *The Oxford handbook of technology and music education*, edited by S. Alex Ruthmann and Roger Mantie, 203–15. New York: Oxford University Press.

———. 2017b. Pondering and end to technology in music education. In *The Oxford handbook of technology and music education*, edited by S. Alex Ruthmann and Roger Mantie, 137–41. New York: Oxford University Press.

Pignato, Joseph M., and Grace Begany. 2015. Deterritorialized, multilocated and distributed: Musical space, poietic domains and cognition in distance collaboration. *Journal of Music, Technology & Education* 8 (2): 111–28.

Pitts, Stephanie. 2011. Discovering and affirming musical identity through extra-curricular music-making in English secondary schools. In *Learning, teaching, and musical identity: Voices across cultures*, edited by Lucy Green, 227–8. Bloomington: Indiana University Press.

———. 2013. *Chances and choices: Exploring the impact of music education.* New York: Oxford University Press.

Powell, B., G. D. Smith, and A. D'Amore. 2017. Challenging symbolic violence and hegemony in music education through contemporary pedagogical approaches. *Education 3–13: International Journal of Primary, Elementary and Early Years Education.* http://dx.doi.org/10.1080/03004279.2017.1347129

Preston, Catherine. 2013. Ryan's not counting—It's eight beats on C: Developing the musician in a classroom context. In *Developing the musician: Contemporary perspectives on teaching and learning*, edited by Mary Stakelum, 209–30. Farnham: Ashgate.

Rabkin, Nick, and E. C. Hedberg. 2011. *Arts education in America: What the declines mean for arts participation.* Washington, DC: National Endowment for the Arts. www.arts.gov/sites/default/files/2008-SPPA-ArtsLearning.pdf

Randles, Clint. 2013. A theory of change in music education. *Music Education Research* 15 (4): 471–85.

Randles, Clint, and David Stringham, eds. 2013. *Musicianship: Composing in band and orchestra.* Chicago, IL: GIA Publishing.

Reay, Diane. 2010. Sociology, social class and education. In *The Routledge international handbook on the sociology of education*, edited by Michael W. Apple, Stephen J. Ball, and Luis Armando Gandin, 396–404. London: Routledge.

Regelski, Thomas. 2002. Musical values and the value of music education. *Philosophy of Music Education Review* 10 (1): 49–55.

———. 2013. Re-setting music education's 'default settings'. *Action, Criticism, and Theory for Music Education* 12 (3): 7–23.

Robson, Colin. 2011. *Real world research.* West Sussex: John Wiley & Sons Ltd.

Schwandt, Thomas A. 2007. *The dictionary of qualitative inquiry.* Thousand Oaks, CA: Sage Publications.

Searle, John. 1983. *Intentionality: An essay in the philosophy of mind.* Cambridge: Cambridge University Press.

———. 1997. *The construction of social reality.* New York: Free Press.

———. 1998. *Mind, language and society.* New York: Basic Books.

Seidman, Irving E. 2006. *Interviewing as qualitative research.* New York: Teachers College Press.

Small, Christopher. 1987. *Musicking: The meanings of performing and listening.* Middletown, CT: Wesleyan University Press.

Smith, Gareth Dylan. 2011. Freedom to versus freedom from: Frameworks and flexibility in assessment on an edexcel BTEC level 3 diploma popular music performance program. *Music Education Research International* 5: 34–45.

———. 2013a. *I drum, therefore I am: Being and becoming a drummer.* Farnham: Ashgate.

———. 2013b. Seeking 'success' in popular music. *Music Education Research International* 6: 26–37.

———. In Press. (Un)popular music making and eudaimonism. In *The Oxford handbook of music making and leisure*, edited by Roger Mantie and Gareth D. Smith. New York: Oxford University Press.

Smith, Gareth Dylan, Mike Dines, and Tom Parkinson, eds. 2017. *Punk pedagogies: Music, culture and learning.* New York: Routledge.

Smith, Jonathan A., Paul Flowers, and Michael Larkin. 2009. *Interpretive phenomenological analysis: Theory, method, and research.* London: Sage Publications.

Söderman, Johan, and Göran Folkestad. 2004. How hip-hop musicians learn: Strategies in informal creative music making. *Music Education Research* 6 (3): 313–26.

Spradley, James P. 1979. *The ethnographic interview.* New York: Harcourt, Brace, Jovanovich College Publishers.

Spruce, Gary. 1999. Music, music education and the bourgeois aesthetic: Developing a music curriculum for the new millennium. In *Learning and knowledge*, edited by Robert McCormick and Carrie Paechter, 71–87. Thousand Oaks, CA: Sage Publications.

Stake, Robert E. 1995. *The art of case study research.* Thousand Oaks, CA: Sage Publications.

Stakelum, Mary, and David Baker. 2013. The maps project: Mapping teacher conceptions of musical development. In *Developing the musician: Contemporary perspectives on teaching and learning*, edited by Mary Stakelum, 135–54. Farnham: Ashgate.

Stålhammar, Börje. 2003. Music teaching and young people's own musical experience. *Music Education Research* 5 (1): 61–8.

Swanwick, Keith. 1988. *Music, mind and education.* London: Routledge.

Tilly, Charles. 1990. How (and what) are historians doing? *American Behavioral Scientist* 33 (6): 685–711.

Tiryakian, Edward A. 1973. Sociology and existential phenomenology. In *Phenomenology and the social sciences*, edited by Maurice Natanson, 187–224. Evanston, IL: Northwestern University Press.

Vogan, Nancy. 2010. Canada: Diverse developments across the decades. In *The origins and foundations of music education: Cross-cultural historical studies of music in compulsory schooling*, edited by Gordon Cox and Robin Stevens, 109–20. London: Continuum.

Waldron, J. 2013. YouTube, fanvids, forums, vlogs and blogs: Informal music learning in a convergent on- and offline music community. *International Journal of Music Education* 31 (1): 91–105.

Williams, David A. 2007. What are music educators doing and how well are we doing it? *Music Educators Journal* 94 (1): 18–23.

———. 2011. The elephant in the room. *Music Educators Journal* 98 (1): 51–7.

Wright, Ruth. 2010. Sociology and music education. In *Sociology and music education*, edited by Ruth Wright, 1–20. Farnham: Ashgate.

Yin, Robert K. 2003. *Case study research design and methods*, 3rd edition. Thousand Oaks, CA: Sage Publications.

About the Authors

Radio Cremata is a composer, keyboardist, and Assistant Professor of Music Education at Ithaca College. He specializes in general and technologically mediated music education. He is an advocate for marginalized communities, underrepresented learners, and non-institutionalized perspectives. The majority of his research centers on celebrations of diversity, innovations in music education, and learner access. Serving in various capacities, he is actively involved in such organizations as the Association for Popular Music Education, the College Music Society, Little Kids Rock, TI-ME, and NAfME.

Joseph Michael Pignato is a composer, improviser, and music education scholar. He holds the position of Professor in the Music Department at the State University of New York, Oneonta, where he teaches courses in music industry, digital music and beat production, and directs ensembles that perform experimental music and improvised rock. Pignato is the leader of Bright Dog Red, an improvising collective that fuses free improvisation, electronica, jazz, hip-hop, psychedelia, and noise music. His research interests include improvisation, alternative music education, and music technology.

Bryan Powell is Director of Higher Education for Little Kids Rock, and Interim Director for Amp Up NYC, a partnership between Berklee College of Music and Little Kids Rock. Bryan is a founding editor of *Journal of Popular Music Education*, a peer-reviewed academic journal published by Intellect Ltd. Additionally, Bryan is Executive Director of the Association for Popular Music Education, an organization dedicated to promoting and advancing popular music at all levels of education. Dr. Powell currently serves as the NAfME Popular Music Education SRIG Chair-Elect.

Gareth Dylan Smith is Manager of Program Effectiveness at Little Kids Rock, New Jersey and Visiting Research Professor at New York University.

He is President of the Association for Popular Music Education, and Chair of the International Society for Music Education's Popular Music Education SIG. Gareth is lead editor of the *Routledge Research Companion to Popular Music Education* and a founding editor of the *Journal of Popular Music Education*. He co-authored, with Hildegard Froehlich, *Sociology for Music Teachers: Practical Applications*, and is lead editor of *Punk Pedagogies: Music, Culture and Learning*. Gareth plays drums with Stephen Wheel, Eruptörs, and Oh Standfast.

Index

For Product Safety Concerns and Information please contact our EU
representative GPSR@taylorandfrancis.com Taylor & Francis Verlag GmbH,
Kaufingerstraße 24, 80331 München, Germany

Printed and bound by CPI Group (UK) Ltd, Croydon, CR0 4YY

11/04/2025

01844009-0019